Speaking and Writing for English Language Learners

Also by Dorit Sasson

Listening and Reading for English Language Learners:
Collaborative Teaching for Greater Success with K–6

Speaking and Writing for English Language Learners

Collaborative Teaching for Greater Success with K–6

Dorit Sasson

ROWMAN & LITTLEFIELD EDUCATION

A division of
ROWMAN & LITTLEFIELD PUBLISHERS, INC.
Lanham • New York • Toronto • Plymouth, UK

Published by Rowman & Littlefield Education
A division of Rowman & Littlefield Publishers, Inc.
A wholly owned subsidiary of The Rowman & Littlefield Publishing Group, Inc.
4501 Forbes Boulevard, Suite 200, Lanham, Maryland 20706
www.rowman.com

10 Thornbury Road, Plymouth PL6 7PP, United Kingdom

Copyright © 2013 by Dorit Sasson

All rights reserved. No part of this book may be reproduced in any form or by any electronic or mechanical means, including information storage and retrieval systems, without written permission from the publisher, except by a reviewer who may quote passages in a review.

British Library Cataloguing in Publication Information Available

Library of Congress Cataloging-in-Publication Data

Sasson, Dorit, 1970-
  Speaking and writing for English language learners : collaborative teaching for greater success with K-6 / Dorit Sasson.
     pages cm
  Includes bibliographical references and index.
  ISBN 978-1-4758-0595-6 (cloth) — ISBN 978-1-4758-0596-3 (pbk.) — ISBN 978-1-4758-0597-0 (electronic) 1. English language—Study and teaching (Elementary—Foreign speakers. 2. English language—Spoken English. 3. English language—Written English. 4. Literacy programs. I. Title.
  PE1128.A2S6323 2013
  372.652'1—dc23
                                                                    2013028325

To Haim Sasson, for his steadfast and loving support and encouragement and for helping me see this book through.

Contents

Acknowledgments ix

Foreword xi

Preface xv

Introduction xix

1 Introduction to Collaboration for K–6 English
  Language Learners 1
  Collaboration past and present, types of collaborative models
  and configurations, benefits of co-teaching and collaboration,
  best practices for collaboration, challenges and obstacles,
  the academic stakes behind collaboration.

2 Collaboration in the Development of Speaking Skills 23
  Obstacles and challenges, developing accuracy and fluency,
  SLA research on error correction and developing accuracy,
  assessing accuracy and meaning through retelling, co-modeling
  conversational strategies, content learning in conversation,
  co-teaching objectives, matching English language proficiency
  standards to language demands, co-teaching discussions on
  content areas, co-teaching situations and models.

3 Collaboration in the Development of Writing Skills 53
  Obstacles and challenges, distinction of the roles between
  English proficiency and English language proficiency, critical

areas of writing, targeted writing skills and standards, supporting co-teaching in writing, vocabulary and SLA influences, strategies for building background knowledge and other schemata, strategies to support writing in content areas, co-teaching situations and models.

Index   81

Acknowledgments

Many, many thanks go out to all the teachers who spent much of their free time speaking to me about their experiences collaborating with other teachers for the sake of ELL students and sharing their resources for the benefit of other teachers. Their support has been invaluable from the start. A big heartfelt thanks to my agent, Bertrand Linder, for believing in the vision of this book from the very beginning and helping me find a home for it. And a big shout of thanks to ELL teacher Kelly Grucelski, who offered invaluable feedback on the book's later drafts and helped make the pages shine.

Foreword

> The process of English language learners acquiring English literacy is not a mere process of learning the linguistic codes. Rather, the process is dynamic, cultural, and social, and it involves not just the learner but, equally important, the teacher, the text, and the context.
>
> —S. Xu (2003), p. 67

The need to support ELL students within schools to insure their success is of critical importance to U.S. educators. There are certainly many configurations to support ELLs within schools such as bilingual education classes or English-language-learning support outside of the classroom. However, most mainstream classroom teachers have the primary responsibility for developing students' competence in English and literacy (Au, 2002; Neufeld & Fitzgerald, 2001). Surprisingly many teachers have had little or no professional development focused on facilitating ELLs' English learning and literacy development (Hadaway, Vardell, & Young, 2004). For this reason and others, many teachers find meeting their ELLs' learning needs a challenge. They worry about how to teach a student who does not speak the language of the school.

    The centrality of language to learning is an issue that teachers of ELLs wrestle with as they provide instruction. A common situation for many ELLs is, upon entry into school, typically preschool or kindergarten, they are expected to only communicate through a new language: English. These students are often expected to achieve the same literacy competencies as their peers who come to school with a home language of English. Very few of these students ever have extra time in school to learn about reading and writing in English as they learn English and how to read and write. They are typically allotted the same amount of time as students who come to school familiar with English to meet grade-level expectations. This is an enormous challenge for students, teachers, and parents (Nieto, 2000).

Dorit Sasson's book is written directly to teachers in mainstream classes who instruct students whose home language is not English. She grounds her book in the idea of the importance of teachers working collaboratively so "they possess more of an ownership to ensure positive results." She acknowledges that many teachers work with ELLs without professional support. Rather than just letting teachers languish with these circumstances, she has created a book that directly supports teachers and provides numerous ways for them to instruct their students in literacy learning.

The first chapter of her book suggests the importance of collaboration and provides ways for teachers to establish collaborative networks within their school. She doesn't just talk about the importance of collaboration; she offers practical suggestions of how to create these partnerships. Building from this chapter, she moves to a discussion of the importance of oral language and reading within language arts instruction and discipline-based instruction. Her next chapter considers writing instruction and how to provide scaffolding for ELLs.

The strength of Sasson's book is that she suggests practical ways to support ELLs. She moves beyond theory to the day-to-day expectations of classrooms. Her work suggests that teachers have high expectations for ELLs so that they can succeed in U.S. classrooms. In today's schools, a general-education teacher needs to understand how to work with ELL students in the classroom with or without ESL professional support (Barone & Xu, 2008). Her book does exactly that—it offers teachers numerous ways to instruct ELLs in language and literacy.

Diane Barone
University of Nevada, Reno

REFERENCES

Au, K. (2002). Multicultural factors and the effective instruction of students of diverse backgrounds. In A. E. Farstrup & S. J. Samuels (Eds.), *What research has to say about reading instruction* (3rd ed., pp. 392–413). Newark, DE: International Reading Association.

Barone, D., & Xu, S. (2008). *Literacy instruction for English language learners in the primary grades.* New York: Guilford Press.

Hadaway, N., Vardell, S., & Young, T. (2004). *What every teacher should know about English learners.* Boston: Pearson/Allyn & Bacon.

Neufeld, P., & Fitzgerald, J. (2001). Early English reading development: Latino English learners in the "low" reading group. *Research in the Teaching of English, 36*, 64–105.

Nieto, S. (1999). *The light in their eyes: Creating multicultural learning communities.* New York: Teachers College Press.

Xu, S. (2003). The learner, the teacher, the text, and the context: Sociocultural approaches to early literacy instruction for English language learners. In D. Barone & L. Morrow (Eds.), *Literacy and young children: Research-based practices* (pp. 61–82). New York: Guilford.

Preface

The Need for This Book

For more than a few years now, there has been a need for this kind of book. In today's day and age, a general-education teacher needs to understand how to work with English language learner (ELL) students in the classroom with or without English as a second language (ESL) professional support, including the culture, the contextual factors of the school, and the legal underpinnings of dealing with ELL students.

With changing demographics and increased globalization worldwide, schools are at a crossroads in terms of how to reduce the achievement gap of K–12 ELL students across the country and especially at the secondary level. Teacher leaders most committed to social justice and inclusive practices (Theoharis, 2009) willingly work with their colleagues to enhance instruction for ELL populations, in many cases with little or no guidance or support from administration. In the current economic climate of budget cuts and teacher job loss, teachers lack a system to support academic needs and progress of their students and commitment to teacher leadership. Collaboration is now a tool for discussion, intervention, and support for ELL students before achievement gaps become too wide.

For the last few years, collaboration has been making strong ripples in the educational community. However, it is still not implemented in many districts and teachers are often discouraged from deviating from curriculum content. Clearly, there needs to be more support and time carved out for teachers to discuss concerns and plan lessons. In fact, research shows that teachers are more likely to outperform expectations and rise to the challenges when they are given the right conditions to collaborate.

Teachers across the country have already started to ride "this wave" by learning more of the positive benefits of collaboration for ELL students. Some teachers already are beginning to take matters in their own hands by dialoguing with other teachers in their schools to create the "ideal leadership" they envision for the twenty-first century. Others just starting their teaching careers need guidance and support in understanding how collaboration can ultimately benefit them and their students. Either way, it takes great faith, courage, and tenacity to begin and stick with a collaborative journey.

Now with the Common Core State Standards (CCSS) initiative, teachers and schools are challenged to implement the CCSS in English language arts (ELA) and mathematics with English language learners. Content-area teachers specifically need guidance as to how ELL students can meet these standards. To this end, school districts will need to provide necessary support for their ESL programs including a formalized ESL curriculum that needs to be established and aligned with the mainstream curriculum using the CCSS to help ELL students academically progress.

A solution to these challenges is in collaborative practices among ESL and content teachers, as well as co-taught classes. States like California, for example, have added about 15 percent more standards to those standards, making the need even greater to align content to standard. Teachers who work in a decentralized district will need to examine some of the instruction across content and decide how to share information. The need for collaboration for the sake of English language learners is now greater than ever.

THE INTENDED TARGET AUDIENCE OF THIS BOOK

This book was written primarily for undergraduate and graduate students who either have or will have—somewhere down the path of their teaching careers—struggling readers who are also ELL students.

Secondary readership includes pre-service teachers or teachers in their first or second year of teaching with a specialization in ESL/ELL and/or early childhood education. Veteran teachers who have taught mixed-ability groups and have students struggling with the reading foundations of acquiring a second language will also benefit from this book. Early childhood and preschool teachers working with struggling, at-risk ELL students or lower-performing native speakers can also benefit from the information presented in this book, as more and more ESL teachers are being asked to support pre-k and kindergarten and they need ideas for developmentally appropriate strategies.

Early intervention provides struggling ELL students and struggling readers the support they need in areas of reading and oral instruction. The intention of this book is to provide practical strategies and techniques grounded in theory to help teachers understand assessment, mapping, diagnosis, and various levels of reading proficiency before implementation. For teacher trainers, the information presented in this book can be used to differentiate various approaches for reading, decoding, and content-area literacy.

OTHER TARGET AUDIENCES AND USES

Each state has mandated objectives for pre-service teachers as well as opportunities to participate in professional development, which is also mandated by the district. Teachers involved in professional learning communities who use this resource as a "book study" that meet once a month for the purpose of increasing test scores and student achievement will find the book useful.

This book can also be used as a resource for ideas for "Response to Interventions" teams or problem-solving teams that focus on student achievement.

Undergraduate students who teach in the primary grades would find this book helpful. It addresses collaboration and ELL methodology in a user-friendly text, with templates. There are lots of commonsense ideas for more than ELL students and especially for the lower elementary student who learns visually.

Of course, all readers will benefit from wanting to collaborate more effectively in the instruction, teaching methods and strategies, planning, and assessment in order to address the academic needs of their struggling ELL students.

WHY THIS BOOK IS IMPORTANT

At the end of the day, a teacher wants to know, "How can I do my day more effectively to produce more positive results and outcomes despite my limited time and resources?"

This book takes the approach that even under the strictest time and curriculum constraints, teachers can start small by using one or more of the strategies and techniques listed in each of the chapters to help further a dialogue and increase awareness on collaboration.

The philosophy of this book centers on the idea that the power of collaboration begins with first seeing the "bigger picture." In fact, magic in the classroom can happen when two teachers who face a common problem work together to find a solution. That bigger picture is formed when teachers start believing in the power of collaboration. When starting small, teachers can see the bigger road map of the journey.

This book was written to provide a starting point for that journey and to encourage teachers to use any of the tips or strategies presented here as a way to sensitize them to the value of collaboration and to encourage them to become better skilled at approaching situations with a collaborative eye for the sake of their own professional work and the achievement of their students.

REFERENCES

Teachers of English to Speakers of Other Languages. (1997). *ESL standards for pre-k–12 students*. Alexandria, VA: TESOL.

Theoharis, G. (2009). *The school leaders our children deserve: Seven keys to equity, social justice, and school reform*. New York: Teachers College Press.

Introduction
What This Book Does and Doesn't Do

This book was "born" from the premise that when teachers are part of collaborative planning, they possess more of an ownership to ensure positive results. This book offers important background information on some of the most important challenges in supporting ELL students academically in various educational contexts and how teachers can use collaboration to address these needs and concerns.

In this book, you will learn how to use collaborative teaching practices to academically support your students in the skill sets of speaking and writing. The chapters take on an integrated skill approach in the area of content. For example, providing opportunities for ELL students to talk about academic texts in math and science can also lead to better reading comprehension. By using conversational and oral reading strategies, co-teachers can also pre-teach academic and subject-specific vocabulary with a cross-disciplinary focus that helps ELL students think and talk about content-area concepts, ask and answer questions, and discuss related themes and concepts.

In both chapters, you'll find descriptions and key concepts of various collaborative contexts for the benefit of English language learners. ELL students enter classrooms with a variety of cultural backgrounds from formal schooling to prevailing cultural attitudes about group work and the role of the teacher.

Teachers need to learn all they can about providing language, literacy, and content to ELL students in diverse settings in order to prevent teacher isolation and gaps in quality instruction. Teachers new to collaboration for ELL students will want to maximize their collaboration to provide the most effective instruction in *all* skill sets. If teachers want to emphasize collaboration as an essential skill for bringing about much-needed educational and social change, they need to maximize their own resources as much as possible. This book, therefore, focuses on the various collaborative models and configurations that will help guide teachers on this journey.

Getting ELL students to academically succeed requires a collaborative effort between the language professional and the regular education teacher. This implies that administration *must* be on board to support both endeavors. However, the complex issue of administrative support is *not* the focus of this book. The issue of administrative support varies from district to district and greatly depends on the quality of school leadership.

Not many teachers are able to fully enjoy the benefits of collaboration when an administration lacks the vision and leadership needed for collaboration to thrive. Therefore, rather than discuss what teachers should do to change the focus of school administrations for the benefit of collaboration, chapter 1 will discuss collaboration from a general perspective of school leadership.

Depending on state requirements, language and reading acquisition for ELL students and how their needs differ from native speakers may be the only information undergraduates get on second language acquisition. In this respect, this book addresses several key areas pre-service and practicing teachers need to know as part of the second-language-acquisition process.

THE ORGANIZATION OF THIS BOOK

This book is grade specific and primarily targets the ELL population. The chapters are organized around skill sets and each chapter provides instructional strategies teachers can use to enhance their collaboration for the sake of academic progress in ELL students.

Chapter Descriptions

Chapter 1 provides an overview on collaborative models and configurations, best practices for collaboration, the challenges and obstacles, the academic stakes behind collaboration, as well as a history of collaboration both past and present.

Chapter 2 provides co-teaching models to support speaking across content areas, obstacles and challenges in teaching speaking, second language acquisition issues such accuracy and fluency and error correction, creating co-teaching objectives and language tasks in speaking across content areas, and matching English-language proficiency standards to language demands. Various co-teaching situations and models will be explored.

Chapter 3 provides co-teaching models to support writing in the four core subjects, activating background and academic knowledge, co-developing prewriting and authentic writing tasks, challenges and problems, co-planning meaningful writing, and using literature-based writing in co-teaching lessons. Various co-teaching situations and models will be explored.

THE PURPOSE

There are several purposes of this book, which include:

- to define academic language development and academic content in the context of team-teaching on K–6 levels;
- to explore how teacher collaboration and co-teaching can provide an effective platform for integrating language, literacy, and content from kindergarten to grade 6;
- to address how teachers can collaborate to make content instruction comprehensible to ELL students at the various levels of language proficiency;
- to show how collaborative practices can support the continuum of academic language development along with reading comprehension, speaking, and writing;
- to show how collaborative practices can support the challenges of supporting reading comprehension at the K–2 and 3–6 levels using real-life scenarios;
- to define teacher collaboration, collaborative team-teaching, and co-teaching in the context of academic support for ELL students; and
- to establish a vehicle for professional development toward creative collaboration between ESL and general-education teachers.

HOW TO USE THIS BOOK

Each chapter focuses on collaborative practices of co-teaching with specialists including the ESL and reading teacher to support reading, speaking, and writing in an academic context as well as both formal and informal collaborative practices. The chapters are structured in a similar fashion for consistency. Recurring features are intended to provide easy access to the content of the book.

- Overview: Each chapter begins with a descriptive preview by emphasizing the key ideas.
- Chapter Questions: With the exception of chapter 1, each chapter starts with two to four questions based on research principles of language learning and teaching that supports collaboration.

- Best Practices in the Classroom: Each chapter includes several authentic classroom and teacher snapshots designed to show collaboration in action and how co-teachers were able to bring the strategies of teaching the skill and/or strategy to life.
- Summary: At the conclusion of each chapter, there are brief recaps of the main ideas and their implications for teaching and collaboration.
- Study Group Discussion Questions: Chapters 2 and 3 provide critical-thinking questions designed to take the understanding to a higher level.
- Activities for Further Collaboration: Chapters 2 and 3 provide opportunities to discuss the topic in more detail, applying the ideas to an everyday practical scenario.
- Web Sources: Chapter 3 includes a series of content-related links that provide an extension of some of the topics addressed.

TERMINOLOGY USED IN THIS BOOK: A NOTE ON ESL AND ELL TERMINOLOGY

In this book, the acronym *ELL* will be used as all-inclusive regardless of the type of program or the grade level—specifically, *ELL* will refer to an ELL student or students to avoid generic labeling. Although there are many different ways to refer to an ELL student's level of proficiency in English, in this book the levels developed by TESOL (Teachers of English to Speakers of Other Languages) will be used: level 1—starting; level 2—emerging; level 3—developing; level 4—expanding; and level 5—bridging. Such standards guide teachers in establishing the knowledge and skills their students need to acquire. Teachers can use these standards to write goals stating what they want their students to know at the end of a lesson or unit of instruction.

To talk about an ELL's native language, the term *L1* will be used, and to talk about his/her second or additional language, English, the term *L2* subsequently will be used.

To date the current educational settings of ELL students, there is also a need to distinguish between an ESL support group and general-education classroom as well as the collaborative contexts for ELLs as either English as a second language (ESL) or general education (GE).

ESL (English as a second language) is an older term that has fallen out of favor because some students may be learning English as their third language. *ELL* (English language learner) is now the preferred term. However, for purposes of identifying collaborative roles and responsibilities in conjunction with the general-education and content-area teachers, the term *ESL teacher* will be used to refer to the language professionals and the ELL students as those children who work directly with an ESL teacher and as the same students in the general-education or mainstream classrooms.

Chapter One

Introduction to Collaboration for K–6 English Language Learners

In the past, the focus of collaboration was on the needs of special-education students in general-education classrooms. In today's academic environment, collaborating for the sake of ELL students is a "must" if teachers want to close academic gaps in content-area literacy in ELL students from kindergarten. Enhancing collaborative partnerships benefits all involved in the process. However, there are still limited opportunities in today's academic environment for all who are involved in the teaching of ELL students to collaborate, leaving teachers to work on their own or seek collaborative resources outside the district.

Teachers continue to face ongoing challenges with time, money, and issues of school leadership that often get in the way of effective collaboration. However, in the long run, teacher collaboration may yield the most effective instruction to meet the diverse academic and language development needs of ELL students. This chapter will focus on the history of collaboration, obstacles, and the various models that are currently being used in today's classrooms to build collaboration and knowledge.

In this chapter, the following topics will be covered:

- an introduction to the different collaborative practices and co-teaching arrangements, promising practices that are emerging as a result of teacher collaboration such as instructional and non-instructional collaborative practices among ESL and mainstream teachers; and
- a history of collaboration and how it has been used in the special-education classroom.

HISTORY OF COLLABORATION—PAST AND PRESENT

Dorit Sasson was an ESL teacher and Tracie Heskett was a general-education teacher in the same school. Both teachers had considerable numbers of ELL students in their class. Meeting the diverse needs of Tracie's ELL students meant constantly finding interesting and successful ways to keep them on task. Dorit needed to ensure that her struggling ELLs were also acquiring word/text-based skills in an ESL context.

The common thread that links both Dorit and Tracie's work is in instructing struggling ELL students—some of whom study with both teachers. In Tracie's general-education class there were several ELL students. In Dorit's ESL class the emphasis was on learning the language. Both teachers had some common planning time to interact professionally to discover the best approaches to working with struggling ELL students in both educational settings, thus allowing them to build partnerships. This type of relationship most represents the general picture and classroom reality of many teachers in schools across the nation.

COLLABORATION—PAST AND PRESENT

Historically, special-needs children in the United States were not part of the regular educational day, and moreover, regular education and special education teachers did not collaborate. Before 1997, the law did not include a regular education teacher as a required member of the Individualized Education Program (IEP) team. Under the 1997 Individuals with Disabilities Education Act, the IEP team for each child with a disability now must include at least one of the child's regular education teachers if the child is or may be participating in the regular education environment. The new law also states that the regular education teacher, to the extent appropriate, participates in the development, review, and revision of the child's IEP.

As can be seen with English language learners, collaborating for the sake of special education students implies that special education students would receive support, instruction, and educational standards from regular education teachers. In this respect, collaboration between special-education teachers and regular education teachers can take different forms. Some special-education students have a team of educators, instructors, therapists, and specialists working with them to guarantee the most successful results. These students may be in a regular education classroom with a regular education teacher for most of the day and then get pulled out of the room for a few hours to complete work with a special-education teacher.

Other students may have a special-education teacher in the regular education classroom with them, working closely with the regular education teacher in a sort of co-teaching model. Similarly to English language learners, the special-education teacher generally modifies the curriculum of the classroom to best support the special-education student, sometimes pulling him out to a quiet area to read or take a test, sometimes spending extra time with him to complete assignments, and often modifying work to meet the requirements of the student's IEP.

PRESENT-DAY COLLABORATION FOR ELL STUDENTS

In today's educational environment, the same collaborative framework used for special-education students also exists for teachers of ELL students. Collaboration is mainly implemented in school districts that have access to resources and funding to support collaborative practices and various pilot programs.

If teachers are to collaborate effectively for the sake of ELL students in today's academic environment, rigorous guidelines and policies need to be implemented and funding must be appropriated. Committees must meet to discuss academic outcomes. In order to place ELL students on an equal playing field for future learning and continued growth that will allow them to compete in an ever-changing and technological world, general-education and other specialized teachers must collaborate. The topic of collaboration needs to be put on national agendas.

While the No Child Left Behind Act (2001) opened a door for rethinking how to diversify teaching methods, learned practices, and materials so that they appeal to a wide variety of learning styles and abilities typical of many ELL classrooms today, teachers still need guidelines in place to support ELL students' academic progress and achievement. This can only work if there is administrative and national support for collaboration to take place.

Collaboration for the sake of special-education students was recognized for one main reason: teachers worked together to fulfill the requirements of an IEP around inclusion-based issues of students of special needs in general-education classrooms. Fulfilling the rigorous requirements of an IEP requires an in-depth knowledge of the curriculum as teachers provide academic, emotional, and social support of special-education students in general-education classrooms. School districts continue to work with administrators and teachers to implement various models and educational frameworks to support the instructional delivery of these students. For the sake of collaboration, teachers are expected to cover a great deal of academic content in diverse classroom settings while they're also expected to integrate ELL students academically.

WHY TEACHERS MUST COLLABORATE

If collaborative frameworks accommodate the rate by which ELL students are absorbed into the general-education classrooms and the degree to which they are expected to understand content-area texts, ELL students would have a greater chance at academic success. Some demographic projections show that 40 percent of the school-age population in the United States will be ELL students by the year 2030 (NWREL, 2004).

Research shows that English language learners represent the fastest-growing student group in U.S. schools, with enrollment increasing more than 150 percent since 1990 (NCELA, 2006). This will put more pressure on teachers to account for their academic progress. In many cases, ELL students show up in regular education classes and it falls on general-education teachers to provide almost all instruction, sometimes with the aid of an ESL professional, but many times without.

This ongoing increase has impacted the way in which national ELL experts and educators view ELL proficiency and how they view the relationship between academic language and content. Through a blog post on *Education Week* (August 16, 2011), national ELL experts and educators are working toward a new direction whereby they are leaving behind the assumption that standards alone guide teachers in establishing what knowledge and skills their students need to acquire, and are currently creating a framework of the English-language demands within the Common Core standards for math and English language arts, as well as for the National Research Council's next-generation science standards.

Between now and the end of 2013, a team of teachers and researchers will analyze the academic language required in different content areas and develop an open-source platform of resources to help teachers of English language learners implement the new standards. Kenji Hakuta, who is spearheading the project, states, "We're not trying to develop standards per se, but we are trying to call attention to the fact that language undergirds much of instruction and learning for all students and especially for English learners. We need to be very aware of the language basis for academic content" (para. 7).

Projections indicate that in two decades this demographic group will comprise more than one-third of students in U.S. schools. Yet the dropout rate continues to grow. An important implication for collaboration that is emerging from these new developments confirms the need for teachers to define as part of their planning how academic language goals will be met based on ELL students' proficiency in academic language of a specific content area and the extent to which teachers integrate a balanced instructional approach in their collaboration.

To place ELL students on an equal playing field for future learning and continued growth that will allow them to compete in an ever-changing and technological world, general-education and other specialized teachers must collaborate. Enhancing collaborative partnerships benefits all students, teachers, and the school community. However, obstacles such as money, time, and school leadership continue to pose a problem to all stakeholders involved in the academic success for ELL students.

OBSTACLES TO COLLABORATION

So why isn't collaboration being implemented in all school districts that have English language learners—even in those districts that have a small number of ELL students? The three biggest reasons are:

- resources and funds,
- school leadership, and
- curriculum and time constraints.

The Problem of Funds and Other Resources

Currently, when states are cutting funds for K–12 programs as well as higher education, administrators tend to think that collaboration between teachers is an expense they cannot afford. In today's academic learning environment, money has become an excuse for hiring and firing teachers as well as curtailing expenses, resources, funding, and other programs.

School Leadership: Coping with the Classroom Realities of Time and Curriculum Constraints

Time Constraints

One of the assumed goals of collaboration for special-education students is that teachers work to better meet the academic needs of their students. However, in order to involve all the stakeholders, schools require appropriate funds, resources, and time for teachers to collaborate. The ESL teacher alone does not have the time to teach all the required content-area vocabulary students need for success! If schools, for example, want ELL students to be on an equal playing field alongside native English speakers, they must invest in pilot-based collaboration-based programs with tailored agendas to meet academic needs.

Lack of time is a reality of classroom life. However, school leaders also need to recognize the importance for teachers to be able to interact with each other on a weekly or daily basis to discuss students' needs and for teachers to plan together. Equally important is scheduling time for administrators and teachers to meet together. In light of this situation, leadership time and funding are all inextricably connected when it comes to support collaboration.

In the article "The Missing Link in School Reform" (2011), Carrie R. Leana states that principals are more successful in producing achievement gains when they focus on providing resources to help teachers build connections as opposed to mentoring and monitoring teachers. If administrators and principles invest in "social capital" (para. 4), or the qualities of building trust and closeness and learning from their conversations with others, teachers will become better in their field of expertise.

True reform efforts happen when trust and meaningful communication among teachers lead to frequent discussions around areas of instruction that ELL students seem to struggle with the most. Based on the results from the survey distributed to more than 1,500 kindergarten to fifth-grade New York City teachers, Leana notes, "If a teacher's social capital was just one standard deviation higher than the average, her students' math scores increased by 5.7 percent" (para. 19).

In a district-wide context that supports collaboration, teachers are given *time* to collaborate. Dove and Honigsfeld (2010) equate a strong administration who believes in collaboration with positive school culture and "play a critical role in providing the human and material resources necessary for teacher collaboration and co-teaching practices to develop and thrive" (p. 139).

For example, a special-education and ESL teacher can discuss a co-teaching plan by sharing with the administration some of the problems and creative solutions for finding time to collaborate. Teachers can share the frustrations of not having a planning-hour block to sit with a crew of special-education teachers and intervention specialists so they can benefit from additional instructional support.

Finally, school leadership influences the degree to which teachers and other stakeholders develop partnerships. If ESL teachers and general-education teachers do not have opportunities for professional interaction, the relationship between ESL and general-education teachers may not lend itself to support and collaboration. For instance, the ESL teacher might come into the general-education classroom to help, but may be made to feel like a teacher's aide. Or the ELL students might be separate in another classroom, where they may or may not be learning the same curriculum as their native peers.

Classroom Constraints

Another classroom reality is that of curriculum constraints. In many school districts, teachers are mandated to use a particular curriculum. Administrators in many school districts discourage deviation from the curriculum content so that teachers can cover the required skills. If ELL students do not have the background knowledge and skills, teachers cannot be expected to speed up the curriculum at the expense of the instruction of ELL students.

WHAT ARE THE CONSEQUENCES OF NOT COLLABORATING?

In today's age of collaboration for ELL students, there are many stakeholders of ELL students who require time and resources to collaborate in the planning, instruction, and assessment of ELL students. These include:

- ESL and content teachers;
- ESL and bilingual teachers;
- ESL and resource teachers;
- ESL and classroom/mainstream teachers;
- ESL and special-education teachers;
- ESL program, school, and district administrators; and
- ESL program and curriculum coordinators.

Lack of adequate time or the resources to collaborate will lead teachers and other stakeholders to figure out on their own the best way to academically support ELL students across the content areas. One of the long-term consequences that occur as a result of a lack of support is that schools placed on the Adequate Yearly Progress (AYP) are listed for subgroups not meeting growth in specific learning areas that require content-based instruction of reading comprehension and vocabulary. Consequently, these schools are also targeted for not meeting the same levels of growth other student groups are either meeting or exceeding.

ELL students tend to be one of those cultural groups that may end up on this list that determines the amount funding allocated to them on a federal level and based on No Child Left Behind (2001). The fact that ELL students are not reaching the required reading standards and proficiency calls for additional funding. As a cultural subgroup, ELL students may continue to not meet the same levels of growth because they are constantly targeted. In doing so, they become a statistic and are never completely supported within a school's system. Inevitably, it becomes the teacher's job to find ways to help them succeed academically.

Increasing numbers of struggling ELL students are not reaching academic proficiency by the end of the fourth grade. These learners are later associated with special needs and slow learners, learning-disabled learners, as well as ADHD and ADD learners. In light of this issue, frameworks for collaboration must be in place for the sake of young ELL students in order to support them academically in all content areas of learning.

SUPPORTING K–2 ELL STUDENTS

On a K–2 level of instruction, academic achievement for ELL students implies incorporating language/literacy skills. Since the nature of the demands of reading change over time, monolingual English students need a balanced form of literacy to address literacy as well as language to help them deal with text. Conversely, teachers need co-teaching strategies to emphasize meaning-making in reading and writing by incorporating more language-rich and literacy-rich activities that support academic development across the content areas.

Collaboration in the areas of literacy, language, and content for K–2 ELL students requires:

- knowledge of effective oral reading instruction that promotes vocabulary knowledge and phonological-awareness training;
- knowledge of the decoding process so learners can make connections between ideas while reading; and
- knowledge of effective fluency strategies that at-risk and struggling ELL students need early on in the decoding process.

COLLABORATIVE MODELS FOR ELL STUDENTS

In today's educational world, teachers are put under tremendous pressure to speed up the curriculum at all costs and for all students. In an age of increased accountability and standardized assessments, a collaborative model supports teachers' work within constraints of the curriculum. Collaborative models, which are a system of guidelines usually given to teachers by administration such as team teaching or parallel teaching, can help English language learners succeed academically if teachers integrate literacy, language, and content (Calderon, Slavin, & Sanchez, 2011).

Similar to the inclusion-based setting of special-education students and students of special needs where a team of teachers is responsible for the delivery of instruction and assessment, likewise, team teachers of ELL students will need to make constant modifications and adjustments in the general-education classroom. Recognizing the types of problems and understanding how these models can best cater to the unique needs of ELL students are the first steps to effective collaboration.

The alarming increase of special needs and number of referrals to specialized schools has also paved the way for a greater number of co-teaching or team-teaching classrooms (Malka, 2011). However, collaborative models still need to be integrated in general-education classrooms even where there are a few English language learners. Many of these inclusive classrooms are often staffed by a general-education teacher who spends many hours alone in instructional planning, classroom management, and assessment. These teachers are the best candidates for a supportive ESL co-teaching framework.

USING AN ESL CO-TEACHING FRAMEWORK

Recognizing the value and expertise of an ESL teacher is central to the idea that a partnership between ESL and content-area teachers can impact academic achievement of ELL students. Multiple models of instructional practice in co-teaching have been recommended by Cook and Friend (1995). For some teachers, co-teaching may not be an option if there is no ESL teacher onsite or if teachers lack the necessary preparation for effectively educating this group.

Tracie Heskett, a second-grade general-education teacher, started the school year with several ELL students only to learn there was no ESL specialist onsite. However, she was able to learn from the experiences of other teachers at school and how they worked with their ELL students.

However, in many school districts, one common model that is currently used is the ESL co-teaching model.

Calderon (2011) proposes five main purposes of an ESL co-teaching framework:

- to address the same theme, genre, essential questions, standards, key vocabulary, and reading and writing skills, and building background information and reviewing key concepts;
- to joint plan, which means allocating school time for joint planning;
- to co-develop complementary lessons or materials;
- to map and align the curriculum; and
- to collaboratively assess student work and plan next interventions.

Clara Lee Brown (2005) refers to this kind of interactive onsite support as "direct consulting," where general-education teachers apply their knowledge of the subject-area curriculum and instruction, while the ESL teacher provides knowledge on second-language acquisition issues and teaching strategies (para. 7). As suggested by Calderon (2011), a supportive ESL co-teaching framework provides opportunities for ELL students to be included in aural-oral activities so they can develop academic language skills throughout their schooling years.

In a supportive ESL co-teaching framework, a first-grade teacher, for example, observes a special-education teacher who teaches several groups of students with special needs including ELL students. The special-education teacher becomes familiar with the role of the first-grade teacher through a hands-on experience by supporting and assisting. Together, they enjoy a hands-on learning experience, by sharing materials and planning collectively with a colleague who is equally invested in the students' achievement.

Co-teaching requires introspection, self-questioning, as well as a variety of intrapersonal and communicative skills and strategies including a willingness to not only hear but also truly listen to the other side and be able to effectively verbalize one's professional needs, wants, and goals. First-grade teacher Tara Malka (2011) agrees: "Co-teachers who recognize each other's strengths and capitalize on them are ensuring that their students meet their personalized educational goals" (para. 9).

In a co-teaching environment, teachers are able to cater to the learning needs of ELL students in the following ways:

1. Both teachers direct the class and are in front of the class. The general-education or core teacher teaches content while the ESL teacher provides examples, clarifies, uses visuals, restates, etc.
2. Teachers switch roles 50 percent of class time. The core teacher teaches, and the ESL teacher monitors or assesses students, and then they switch roles.
3. The class is divided in half and both teach the same content to a heterogeneous group. Both teachers are knowledgeable in the areas of teaching vocabulary, reading-comprehension skills, and writing specific to a content area.
4. Turn-taking. The ESL teacher pre-teaches vocabulary while the core teacher presents the concepts. The ESL teacher asks/clarifies questions, elicits summaries from students, and reinforces the use of new vocabulary.
5. Switching. Both teachers teach multiple groups by switching groups every twenty minutes or so.

As teachers become proficient in the various models, they can plan to use a variety of them. The concept or the skill being covered and students' learning styles will inform the model that works best. The following four models described in detail include:

Model #1: Team Teaching

Regardless of the program type or grade level, team teaching can help ELL students achieve academic outcomes. This model consists of both teachers teaching the same students at the same time. Teachers ensure ELL students have success by the quality of instruction, continuous professional development, whole-school structures, and effective leadership that institute team teaching (Calderon, 2011).

Both co-teachers work together and actively share the planning and instruction of content and skills to all students. Both teach the material by exchanging and discussing ideas and concepts in front of learners, facilitate small-group work and student-led discussion, and model appropriate ways of asking questions. For example, one teacher might talk while the other teacher models a read-aloud or writes on a whiteboard.

Benefits of Team Teaching

- Like other models, teachers work closely to reach solutions to issues relating to students such as behavior, motivation, and teaching styles.
- Both teachers have the opportunity to teach all students.
- Additionally, it provides a supportive environment for both teachers and students.

To meet the needs of ELL students using this type of intervention, the general-education teacher prepares special material and activities for ELL students who are still in small groups or are in general-education classes. The material and activities will be on the same subject matter and include some of the same curriculum goals as regular classroom instruction. However, they will be geared to potentially at-risk or struggling students. The content-area or general-education teacher can collaborate with the ESL teacher in preparing such special activities and materials.

There are various configurations that allow maximum collaboration in a team-teaching setup:

- ESL teachers team with general-education teachers.
- RTI tier-2 teachers team up with tier-1 teachers.

- ESL teachers team up with special-education teachers (or RTI tier 3).
- ESL teachers team up with general-education and special-education teachers.

In a co-taught model, teams of teachers also work collaboratively in the same classroom to plan and implement the interventions and share progress-monitoring and data analysis.

Model #2: Additional Structures for Team Teaching: Push In or Pull Out

Pull out and push in are organizational models that support team teaching configurations. There are many classroom environments where general-education teachers do not have the privilege of working with an ESL specialist.

In schools where there is an ESL specialist, ELL students are mainly "pulled out" of general-education classrooms for special instruction in English as a second language. This, however, creates significant stress on the ESL teacher to perform. As Pardini and Zehr note (2006; 2011), unless teachers have successful cooperative planning and organizational techniques to work in teams, the "pull-out" organization will not help close the language gap for the sake of ELL students. For this reason, more teachers across the country are moving away from the "pull-out" model.

Support for Push In

Even though more districts are pulling away from pull-out configurations, the debate continues. Unfortunately, there is no conclusive research on the effectiveness of supporting the relationship between academic gains and proficiency levels. However, there is an added cultural and social advantage when ELL students study with their native English-speaking peers.

As pointed out by Nicole Fernandez, a second-grade ESL teacher who taught in a pull-out context before moving to a push-in: "It has been a challenge for administration to see the positive effects of this program. However, the students have had a positive effect. The ESL students say they like it so much better. They are not lost in class anymore. The general-education students are much more culturally aware and have gained new relationships."

Teachers in this school district reported they were able to coordinate interventions and pre-teaching so ELL students would not experience random instructional events when the school district moved to the push-in model!

Models #3 and 4: Parallel Teaching and Group Models

Two co-teaching models in particular lend themselves to the delivery of scientific-research-based interventions—parallel teaching and the group model.

Parallel Teaching

If a large number of ELL students in a class require the same intervention, the *parallel teaching* model may be best. This model is most effective when there is a need to differentiate reading materials and provide extension activities to one group while re-teaching another group. In this model, one educator delivers the intervention to one group, while the other educator delivers instruction to the other group. The group receiving instruction could be expanding on concepts already learned, reviewing, or using the time for self-selected reading. Groups can be formed according to reading level or learning styles.

Benefits of Parallel Teaching
- The student-teacher ratio is low.
- Students have more opportunities to get help and support.
- Students' responses and knowledge can be more closely monitored.

Large Group/Small Group

When a small number of students in a class need the same intervention, the large-group/small-group model may be best. In this model, one teacher works with a small group (two to five students) who need the intervention, while the other teacher continues instruction with the larger group. This model is used to either re-teach a learning concept or extend learning for a group of students. The main importance is to keep groupings as flexible as possible when transitioning from activity to activity.

This model also works best when implementing intervention with an individual student. Using this model requires much more planning than the parallel model, because the intervention must fit into a time in the day or class period when students can move in and out of the larger group without missing new instruction. A benefit to this model is that it can be used when teachers find it necessary to progress and monitor students.

Benefits
- Teachers have additional instructional time to support struggling students.
- Teachers can provide more individualized instruction and, therefore, build a learning and educational profile of each student.

COLLABORATION ON A WHOLE-SCHOOL STRUCTURE

Many district ESL directors offer some professional development, but these development courses are not subject-specific and ongoing to the needs of

ELL students. To support collaboration for the sake of ELL students, professional development must help all teachers understand second-language acquisition and be able to incorporate new strategies and methodologies including the opportunity to co-teach to improve instruction for ELL students.

ESL program models, collaborative models and roles, teamwork, and structures should frame continuous professional development. Instituting professional development occurs through administrative support, which is the backbone for whole-school support (Calderon, 2011).

For English language learners, the cost of covering the curriculum is greater than usual, as teachers often inadvertently ignore the language needs of these students in content courses. Calderon (2011) recommends that schools strategize and maximize professional development to include all teachers involved in the teaching of ELL students regardless of grade level, subject area, language of instruction, and educational contexts, as revealed in the following examples:

- three-five initial days of professional development where ESL and content teachers participate by grade levels to address specific needs of teachers: kindergarten to grade eighth and ninth- through twelfth-grade cohorts;
- professional development in English and professional development in first language (e.g., Spanish) for bilingual classrooms; and
- refresher workshops during the year for all teachers on all components and as needed.

THE ROLE OF ADMINISTRATION IN CO-TEACHING AND COLLABORATION

Calderon, Slavin, and Sanchez (2011) offer the following eight features to ensure academic success:

- providing time for planning time/collaboration between general-education and ESL teachers;
- scheduling ESL teachers' workload with care;
- grouping ELL students by proficiency levels and no more than two grade levels;
- keeping ESL classes small (below fifteen; ideally ten);
- one ESL teacher per content area (one for math, one for science, etc.);
- providing all necessary resources and materials;
- providing ongoing professional development for general and ESL teachers together; and
- promoting high status for all ELL efforts and respect for team teachers.

The support of administration can also impact the degree to which teachers and many members of staff are engaged in peer coaching and teacher support. For example, coaches and site administrators participate in training for ELL students. General-education and ESL teachers attend workshops on peer coaching and coach each other to improve instruction and learning. Co-teachers observe and document student performance and their co-teacher's instructional delivery. Peers record observations of ELL students or co-teachers.

WHAT DO DIVERSITY STANDARDS IMPLY FOR COLLABORATION?

Since English language learners are also a K–12 issue, teachers need to know how to provide culturally and linguistically responsive instruction that is viewed and addressed as a part of K–12 education. Associations such as the National Association for Bilingual Education (NABE) and the National Council of Accreditation for Teacher Education (NCATE) place a special emphasis on providing "on-grade-level" academic knowledge and skills, which include literacy at the elementary and secondary levels to bilingual learners.

In 2010, the NABE drafted a national action for the education of bilingual learners. The last forty years of research on second-language acquisition in the United States has affirmed the effectiveness of using a child's native language to learn academic concepts while learning the English language. However, schools have yet to catch up with the research, leaving teachers to cope with a consistently growing academic achievement gap between native English speakers and bilingual learners.

A great deal of diversity exists in how schools help teachers approach bilingual learners, as indicated by the Standards for Reading Professionals (2010) and how schools create a diverse environment for collaboration to flourish and grow. One of the assumptions implies collaborating for the sake of providing culturally and linguistically responsive instruction across educational contexts. It identified that "language-minority students need appropriate and different language and literacy instruction if they are to be successful academically while they learn English" (2010).

Similarly, in 2008, standard four of six teacher-education standards developed by the NCATE focused on diversity. For teachers, this means they provide equal access to an academic and linguistic education to help ELL students become "English proficient" and academically on grade level. It states, "Experiences provided for candidates include working with diverse populations, including higher education and P–12 school faculty, candidates, and students in P–12 schools" (2008).

By coming together in their cultural understandings of their diverse learners and deliberately incorporating these conversations in their collaboration, teachers can meet the instructional standards of diversity. Curran (2003) describes that "when teachers learn to see the diverse backgrounds of their students as resources, these students' experiences can serve to promote the multilingualism and multiculturalism of all the students and the teacher" (p. 338).

WORKING WITH LEARNING DISABILITIES IN A COLLABORATIVE CONTEXT

Similarly to those collaborative models that presently serve general-education and special-education teachers for the sake of students with special needs, teachers of ELL students need to be supported in their work with ELL students who may have a learning disability.

In fact, the number of ELL students with learning disabilities has risen so much in many districts that the need for developing strong, collaborative relationships with ESL and bilingual teachers as well as special-education professionals and specialists has become that much more acute. Shah states (2011), "With some states experiencing a 700 percent growth in the number of English learners in their schools between 1994 and 2005, the department expects the number of English Learners with disabilities to increase, too" (para. 1).

However, the problems understanding the issue require knowledge of second-language acquisition and effective interventions. In some districts that do work with ELL students of learning disabilities, a collaborative framework helps teachers facilitate communication in their collaboration. Finding solutions to learning disabilities is challenging especially when teachers have to take into consideration a language barrier, which can complicate the situation (Santos & Ostrosky, n.d.).

When teachers and specialists refer an ELL student to special-education services, is the problem always a learning disability, or is it a second-language acquisition issue? How does intervention play a role in collaboration? Would the special-education support be the kind of help that student needs? How can teachers effectively collaborate for the benefit of these students?

There are no easy answers to these questions. A common thread that emerges from these difficult questions reinforces the need for enhanced communication and cooperation among all teachers who share the responsibility of teaching ELL students who may exhibit signs of a learning disability with the specific target of maximizing what Allington refers to as "instructional expertise" (2011, 173).

In many cases ELL students who have learning disabilities often do not receive the services they need. Their problems may be unrecognized because they are second-language learners. They may be referred to special education but not receive appropriate services because of a lack of bilingual special-education teachers. They are not assessed for learning disabilities because of their lack of English.

Before teachers move too quickly in the direction of special-education referrals, districts need to improve the quality of teacher training for general-education teachers who work with an increasingly diverse student population including English language learners, children from diverse cultural backgrounds, and children living in poverty to help bring awareness and sensitivity to the many variables such as poverty, stress at home, or upheaval due to the immigration process and moving to a new country with a different culture. Additionally, schools can improve general-education strategies by implementing teacher teams to improve instruction that is data driven, is collaborative, and includes schoolwide intervention as well as appropriate language support in teams.

THE INCLUSION MODEL

Inclusion is the best response to the idea that, to the maximum extent possible, students with disabilities are to be educated with their nondisabled peers in the general-education classroom. Whether catering to ELL students or special-needs students in an inclusion-based environment, teachers use their knowledge of co-teaching to help them expand their teaching to include the broadest range of learners.

The inclusion model assumes that all students, regardless of ability, level, or background, will receive research-based, high-quality, differentiated instruction from a general-education teacher in a general-education setting. The objective of differentiated instruction is to maximize each student's growth where he or she is and teaching from that point. The underlying view of differentiated instruction is that "one size does not fit all"—an idea counter to an assumption in many classrooms.

Routinely, the general educator assesses students' progress in the curriculum and makes ongoing adjustment to target the needs of students including those with special needs and English language learners.

CREATING A CO-TEACHING MODEL FOR ELL/LEARNING-DISABLED STUDENTS

Whether co-teachers are instructing ELL students who may be learning disabled or instructing students of special needs in an inclusion-based setting, both special-education teachers and ESL/content teachers will need to work collaboratively in the same classroom to deliver instruction. This collaboration involves jointly developing and agreeing upon a set of common goals, sharing responsibility of obtaining these goals, and working together to achieve these goals using each others' expertise.

ESL Team Teaching

ESL teacher-led teach teams is one way for all teachers of ELL students to discuss language, literacy, and content in an inclusion-based setting. For the delivery of special-education and related services, teachers are encouraged to use a team approach whenever possible led by the ESL teacher in the position as a "direct consultant" (Brown, 2005, para. 9). Other professionals would directly benefit from her/his expertise, especially for those students who need special-education and language support services and thus, they provide time for team planning to collaborate with bilingual/ESL personnel.

Teacher teams include general-education and special-education teachers, paraprofessionals, and building specialists who design the intervention plan at different tiers to discuss the role of second-language acquisition issues and ESL strategies for co-teaching. The problem, however, that teachers continue to face is that the kind of support given to students with reading or language disabilities is not the kind of support that second-language learners need, which, again, reinforces the need for enhanced communication and collaboration among all teachers who share the responsibility of teaching these kinds of ELL students.

When it comes to referring either a struggling or at-risk elementary ELL student to special services or interventions, the expertise of an ESL teacher on the issues of second-language acquisition can be most useful in determining possible treatments. One common cause for referral of these students has to do with misinterpreting the area of error analysis made by second-language learners.

Ellis (2003) raises important points for distinguishing between errors and mistakes. Equally important for teachers to consider is the learner's stage of second-language acquisition particularly regarding a learner's silent period, a developmental pattern where the learner is deeply absorbing the language but is not producing it—largely a feature in communicative settings. In many cases where the "silent period may serve as a preparation for subsequent production" (p. 20), teachers can start the process of classifying grammatical errors early "as a way to help us *diagnose learners' learning problems* at any one stage of their development and, also, to plot how changes in error patterns occur over time" (p. 18).

For example, leaving words out in speech or in writing is an example of the early stages of L2 acquisition. But if these errors persisted in the intermediate stages of second-language learning, teachers may need to evaluate the level of consistency in the learner's performance versus possessing knowledge of the correct form or whether the learner was just slipping up a mistake random to a specific area of producing language in communication.

Second-language acquisition is largely an internal process, and much of which also has to do with mother-tongue interference. As Rod Ellis (2003) states, "Some errors are common only to learners who share the same mother tongue or whose mother tongue manifest the same linguistic property" (p. 19).

Understanding what learners do when exposed to the L2 in communicative settings reveals a great deal of the level of second-language acquisition and what the ESL and general-education teacher can do to further their collaboration:

- diagnosing errors in terms of type, frequency of occurrence, and
- distinguishing passive vs. active production—from a second-language-acquisition point of view, many struggling ELL who exhibit silent behaviors are silent.

To develop an intervention plan that provides struggling readers with more intensive instructional support, teachers need to maximize each teacher's "expertise" and a "decreased classroom size" (Allington, 2011) in order to increase the likelihood of reading acceleration. For the sake of effective collaboration, teachers need to follow specific guidelines to make these interventions effective for second-language learners. Although Allington's principles of intervention refer to struggling readers whose mother tongue is English, all professionals need to provide ELL students who have reading or language disabilities with customized support.

SUMMARY

It is only recently that teacher collaboration for the sake of English language learners is gathering more attention from the educational community. In today's era of high academic stakes and standardized testing, collaboration for the sake of English language learners is necessary for academic success. Collaboration creates a supportive learning environment for teachers and students. When teachers collaborate frequently and consistently, they are able to optimize the learning environments and cope with ongoing challenges.

REFERENCES

Allington, R. L. A. (2011). *What really matters for struggling readers: Designing research-based programs.* Boston: Allyn & Bacon.

August, D. & Hakuta, K. (1997). *Improving schooling for language-minority children.* Washington, DC: National Academy Press.

August, D., & Shanahan, T. (Eds.). (2006). *Developing literacy in second-language learners: Report of the National Literacy panel on language-minority children and youth*. Mahwah, NJ: Erlbaum.

Barone, Diane. (2008, December 8). "Someone I'd Like You to Meet: Professor Diane M. Barone." Interview. *New Teacher Resource Center*. Retrieved December 8, 2008, from http://newteacherresourcecenter.com/?p=537

Brown, C. L., & Bentley, M. (2004). "ELLs: Children left behind in science class." *Academic Exchange Quarterly, 8*(3), 152–157.

Brown, C. L. (2005). "Ways to help ELLs: ESL teachers as consultants." *Academic Exchange Quarterly*. Retrieved December 20, 2010, from http://findarticles.com/p/articles/mi_hb3325/is_4_9/ai_n29236331

Calderon, M. E. (2007). *Teaching reading to English language learners, grades 6–12: A framework for improving achievement in the content areas*. Thousand Oaks, CA: Corwin.

Calderon, M. E., & Minyana-Rowe, L. (2011). *Preventing long-term English language learners: Transforming schools to meet core standards*. Thousand Oaks, CA: Corwin.

Calderon, M. E., Slavin, R. E., & Sanchez, M. (2011). Effective instruction for English language learners. In M. Tienda & R. Haskins (Eds.), *The future of immigrant children*. Washington, DC Brookings Institute/Princeton University.

Cook, L., & Friend, M. (1995). Co-teaching: Guidelines for creating effective practices. *Focus on Exceptional Children, 28*(3), 1–16.

Curran, M. E. (2003). Linguistic diversity and classroom management. *Theory into Practice, 42*(4), 334–340.

DelliCarpini, M. (2008). Teacher collaboration for ESL/EFL academic success. *The Internet TESL Journal, 14*(8). Retrieved January 1, 2011, from http://iteslj.org/Techniques/DelliCarpini-TeacherCollaboration.html

Ellis, R. (2003). *Second language acquisition*. Oxford: Oxford University Press.

Honigsfeld, A., & Dove, M. (2010). *Collaboration and co-teaching: Strategies for English learners*. Thousand Oaks, CA: Corwin.

International Reading Association. (2010). Standards 2010: Standard 4. Retrieved June 6, 2013, from http://reading.org/General/CurrentResearch/Standards/ProfessionalStandards2010/ProfessionalStandards2010_Standard4.aspx

Leana, C. (2011). *The Missing link in school reform*. Stanford Social innovation Review. Retrieved September 1, 2011, from www.ssireview.org/articles/entry/the_missing_link_in_school_reform

Malka, T. (2011, April 14). *Exploring methods of effective co-teaching*. United Federation of Teachers. Retrieved September 6, 2011, from www.uft.org/teacher-teacher/exploring-methods-effective-co-teaching

Manyak, Patrick C., & Bauer, E. B. (2008, February). "Explicit code and comprehension instruction for English learners." *The Reading Teacher, 61*(5), 432–434. Retrieved June 6, 2013, from www.pebc.org/wp-content/uploads/2010/01/Manyak-Explicit-code-comp-inst-20083.pdf

National Association for Bilingual Education. (2010). National action plan for the education of bilingual learners. Retrieved July 25, 2011, from www.nabe.org/files/NABE_NATIONAL_ACTION_PLANS.pdf

National Clearinghouse for English Language Acquisition. (2006). *The growing number of limited English proficient students 1991–2002*. Washington, DC: U.S. Department of Education.

National Council of Accreditation for Teacher Education. (2008). Six teacher education standards. Retrieved July 23, 2011, from www.ncate.org/Standards

Northwest Regional Educational Laboratory. (2004). ELL unit focuses on growing population. NW Report.

Office of English Language Acquisition. (2003). Descriptive study of services to LEP students and LEP students with disabilities. University of Minnesota, National Center on Educational Outcomes. Retrieved June 6, 2013, from www.ncela.gwu.edu/files/rcd/BE021199/special_ed4.pdf

Pardini, P. (2006). In one voice: Mainstream and ELL teachers work side-by-side in the classroom teaching language through content. *Journal of Staff Development, 27*(4), 20–25.

Santos, R. M., & Ostrosky, M. M. (n.d.) Understanding the impact of language differences on classroom behavior. What Works Brief no. 2. Nashville, TN: Center on the Social and Emotional Foundations for Early Learning. Retrieved June 6, 2013, from http://csefel.vanderbilt.edu/briefs/wwb2.pdf

Teachers of English to Speakers of Other Languages. (2007). ESL standards for pre-K–12 students. Retrieved December 17, 2008, from www.tesol.org/s_tesol/seccss.asp?CID=95&DID=1565

U.S. Department of Education. (2006). 28th annual report to Congress on the implementation on the *Individuals with Disabilities Education Act*, vol. 1. Retrieved June 6, 2013, from www2.ed.gov/about/reports/annual/osep/2006/parts-b-c/28th-vol-1.doc

Zehr, Mary A. (2011) Stanford to lead creation of ELL standards for "Common Core." Retrieved July 12, 2011, from, http://blogs.edweek.org/edweek/learning-the-language/2011/07/stanford_to_lead_creation_of_e.html?qs=hakuta

Chapter Two

Collaboration in the Development of Speaking Skills

One of the ways co-teachers can support ELL students at the early stages of second-language learning is by providing opportunities to academically progress in the language domain of speaking. Although many ELL students might feel hesitant to speak in another language, when co-teachers plan effectively, they establish a safe and nonthreatening learning environment.

This chapter will focus on those strategies and techniques co-teachers can use to help ELL students in the area of speaking across the content areas for middle-elementary ELL students. It explores the complexities and challenges in developing the language domain of speaking in K–6 ELL students and provides a direction of how collaboration and co-teaching can lead to better reading. This chapter begins by describing some of the challenges and obstacles in the area of speaking. It also defines critical areas of co-teaching and provides co-teaching scenarios of struggling ELL students.

This chapter will focus on the following questions:

- What are some of the obstacles and challenges for teachers in teaching speaking and how can they address these areas in their collaboration?
- What does second-language acquisition research say in terms of supporting ELL students in the language domain of speaking?
- What are some of the ways co-teachers can promote young ELL students' language production across academic content areas?
- How can ESL and content-area co-teachers promote the use of speaking across content areas?

WHAT ARE SOME OF THE OBSTACLES AND CHALLENGES IN TEACHING SPEAKING?

Teaching speaking in content-area classrooms makes it easier for ELL students to academically progress in the area of reading. Research shows that ELL students need academic and content-specific language for success. Students need regular opportunities to talk and use academic vocabulary and discourse to make concepts their own and to internalize the new ways of expressing ideas (Echevarria, Vogt, & Short, 2004; Marzano, 2004; Shanahan & Beck, 2007).

However, acquiring speaking proficiency is one of the hardest skills for ELL students to achieve. At the beginning stages of second-language acquisition, students are often "stuck in the middle ground of being conversational in English, but lacking in the breadth of English needed for content area success" (Ogle & Correa-Kovtun, 2010). These concerns are well documented in the professional literature as challenges for schools across this country (August, Carlo, Dressler, & Snow, 2005; Fitzgerald, Amendum, & Guthrie, 2008; Lesaux & Geva, 2006; Mora, 2009).

Spoken language is an area of competence in its own right, to be fostered alongside other aspects of the language curriculum (Stierer & Maybin, 1994). For instance, ELL students may appear to be proficient when talking on the playground with friends, but they need to move beyond basic interpersonal communication skills to learn the academic and disciplinary language required to be successful in reading, writing, and talking in science (Cummins & Swain, 1986).

To this end, ELL students often enter general-education classrooms fluent in conversational skills. However, many children who speak English as a second or third language possess less extensive English academic vocabulary, which often poses a hurdle when reading informational texts, a challenge that is particularly frustrating when reading social studies and science texts.

Research shows that reading comprehension that is supported by speaking bridges gaps between learning and deeper understanding. When it comes to learning academic vocabulary across the content areas, for example, ELL students need scaffolded classroom talk to deepen their understanding of texts (Wolf, Crosson, & Resnick, 2004). Cummins (1986) explains that conversational English develops quite rapidly for ELL students, generally within two to three years, but academic language takes much longer. To this end, co-teachers can include speaking opportunities for ELL students to connect language and content, which is often missing in the content-area curriculum.

ELL students need opportunities to talk and use academic vocabulary and discourse to make concepts their own and to internalize the new ways of expressing ideas (Echevarria, Vogt, & Short, 2004; Marzano, 2004; Shanahan & Beck, 2007). Providing guidance and feedback to students' output using English in meaningful and communicative contexts is crucial if teachers want to effectively increase students' oral English production.

CHALLENGES WITH SUPPORTING YOUNG ENGLISH LANGUAGE LEARNERS

Lastly, young ELL students who are at the beginning stages of language acquisition may not have an understanding of the syntax of the English language to extend their discourse. Typically, young English learners struggle with core curricula because they lack academic vocabulary knowledge. In a co-teaching framework, teachers can address lesson materials and strategies for explicit and interactive instruction of vocabulary with an ESL context to prepare lower-level English learners for the demands of content-area lessons.

Challenges of Developing Accuracy and Fluency

Another challenge for developing the language skill of speaking is monitoring and evaluating the progress of speaking, particularly in the areas of fluency and accuracy, or promoting form vs. meaning, while also taking into account the stages of second-language acquisition.

During a recent TESOL webinar entitled "The Fluency Paradox Revisited" (2011), Jeremy Harmer discusses the implications of accuracy and fluency in a communicative-language context. When discussing fluency, one is typically referring to *natural language use* and *the imitation of native speaker use*. In the traditional accuracy-based understanding of second-language learning and acquisition, the teacher's role has always been to focus on evaluation of accuracy and provide more guided activities that promote accuracy.

In the article "Communicative Methodology in Language Teaching," Brumfit (1984) explores the ongoing debate in light of the argument that not all classroom instructional strategies lend themselves to supporting accuracy. To this end, teachers may need to revisit accuracy-aimed activities and ask questions about the role of fluency versus accuracy in content-based activities, which may also prompt teachers to accelerate oral progress.

Accelerating Oral Progress

In various formal and informal assessment situations where teachers are faced with ELL students who score substantially below grade level or want to help

ELL students when they encounter difficulty, teachers may need to make instructional decisions and adaptations to accelerate student progress, which also impacts co-teaching environments. Because most of the teaching tends to stop at the practice level, teachers need to integrate lots of guided practice in the areas of fluency and accuracy.

Recent research shows that students' speaking plays a crucial role in the acquisition of reading fluency and comprehension (Nation & Snowling, 2004; Pullen & Justice, 2003). When ELL students are new to learning a targeted form, providing guided oral forms of practice is crucial for supporting the acquisition stage of "chunking" (Ellis, 1994). One way co-teachers can accelerate student progress is by planning guided and semi-guided oral forms of practice that are teacher-oriented and directed. For example, one teacher may say, "I cooked the dinner," (teacher-oriented) or provide a "clue" to generate student response (semi-guided practice) as in the example: "What did you do last night?"

What Does the Research Say about Accuracy and Correcting Mistakes?

One of the major questions that arise when discussing accuracy and fluency is "how important is it for ELL students to be accurate in their language use?" First, it is necessary to identify "accurate" or "correct" usage and whether error correction helps and, if so, what kinds are most effective. From the point of view of the listener or reader, "accuracy," even if it doesn't affect meaning, is "discourteous" and "distracting." It may also lower respect for the speaker or writer.

From the point of view of the speaker or writer, inaccuracy may lower self-confidence and self-respect as a language user. Finally, from the point of view of the language teacher, professionalism means teaching the language as best as can be.

Jenkins (2006) writes,

> Despite the accumulating evidence against IL (interlanguage) theory, the literature on teaching English still regularly contains advice for teachers in both outer and expanding circles on how to reduce IL errors and how to reverse fossilization…there is still little if any awareness among TESOL practitioners and SLA researchers that learners may be producing forms characteristic of their own variety of English, which reflect the sociolinguistic reality of their English use, whatever their circle, far better than either British or American norms are able to do. (168)

In the context of English as a lingua franca, there is such a thing as "correct" and "incorrect" and "acceptable" and "unacceptable." For example, "she go" would be considered as a legitimate "variant" and not as "incorrect."

Given the fact that teachers do not have time to teach everything, one approach would be to prioritize the top five language errors. One benefit would stem from the need to create a clear basis for classroom teaching, materials design, and tests as well as teaching ELL students the most useful, acceptable, and important forms used for English worldwide. These "variants" also may not be acceptable for the students' own emergent language production. When learners use "incorrect" or "unacceptable" forms, teachers should probably correct them.

Best Practices in the Classroom

One of the major obstacles and challenges that has arisen for co-teacher Kelly Grucelski is error correction. In light of her ELL students' spoken English, she says, "As a listener, I have to work very hard to understand what my students are saying. It's a constant struggle. For example, they might say, "I didn't went to Walmart," or not address her appropriately with the correct title as "Ms. Grucelski."

However, she has found that even with her students' errors, she can still communicate with them and understand the gist of what they are saying. For example, she mentions that if she and her co-teacher were to make error correction a priority, they would first need to identify common cultural and linguistic errors that stem from not knowing how to address a teacher as well as linguistic errors that do not distinguish between "telling" and "asking." She also suggests the idea of "morning meetings," where ELL students discuss what they did over the weekend or after school.

In their co-teaching, they would correct some of the spoken output using direct instruction and co-modeling, allowing their students to have more opportunities to hear the correct word forms and meanings.

Assessing Accuracy and Meaning through Retelling

The strategy of retelling, which is similar to summarizing, requires ELL students to capture the main idea or problem, all significant events or information, and as many relevant details orally. "Not only is retelling an important comprehension strategy but also it enhances language development and communication skills" (MacDonald & Figueredo, 2010).

In their assessments, co-teachers will want to decide on their weight of various areas of content, depending on the incoming levels of spoken language and reading comprehension and how well they are acquiring English over time. For example, they may wish to assess how well students retold the main idea of problem, all significant events, information, and details as well as sequence and coherence. The following activities prepare ELL students for the procedure of retelling.

Oral Reading Activities

ELL students read/record orally the sentences or parts of a story that include multiple sets of previously introduced core words. Encourage ELL students to "rehearse" a story or text before beginning to draw or write it. For example, if students are going to draw a text, they can "rehearse" it by telling the most important idea of a section of a text, distinguishing it from details that tell more about it. Ideally, this can be done in pairs.

Picture Concept Sorts

Teachers use pictures of objects, places, and people to help students "try out" or "play" sorting different groups in their own way. Students can manipulate, talk about, and try various groupings of the objects.

Connecting Vocabulary Activities with Speaking

Students create their own mini-books of the book using themed vocabulary, ABC words, or the language of sentence frames to provide the text. They then read the text aloud to their partners.

Connecting Writing Activities with Speaking

Have students get to know a partner and fill in the blanks. Examples:

1. My partner speaks _____ and _____
2. My partner plays _____
3. My partner reads _____
4. My partner's favorite subject is_____
5. My partner's favorite food is_____

CO-MODELING CONVERSATIONAL STRATEGIES

The strategy of asking and answering questions around academic content encourages ELL students to talk and ask questions as they interact with their native English-speaking peers and their teachers. Co-modeling open-ended questions can also serve as a scaffold for questioning that will help students think about the kinds of questions that will stimulate discussion. Co-teachers may find they need to model and reinforce these oral routines to support conversation as they engage students in conversation without "letting the conversation end with one response" (Wasik, 2010).

Asking open-ended questions (i.e., questions that require more than a yes/no response) has been documented as an effective technique for providing opportunities for children to use language (Dickinson & Smith, 1994; Whitehurst et al., 1988).

Using the PRC2 to Co-teach Content Learning in Conversation

Research has shown that ELL students need ongoing opportunities to help navigate academic content prior to speaking about it. Ciechanowski (2009) recommends explicitly "connecting each variety of English to its appropriate contexts and purposes, such as teaching and learning science, rather than teach separate or disconnected vocabulary or grammar lessons" (p. 561).

For co-teachers, this implies how to coordinate each other's efforts so that ELL students understand the "differences and similarities in language used across every day, academic, and disciplinary texts—not only textbooks but also trade books and student-chosen everyday texts, as well" (p. 561). To implement these research-based ideas in speaking contexts, co-teachers can provide opportunities for students to practice text reading or develop a greater understanding of the key vocabulary without orally presenting them.

One of the oral routines that has been successfully used with young ELL students is PRC2 (Ogle & Correa-Kovtun, 2010), referred to as "Partner Reading and Content, Too," which involves monitoring the interaction of student pairs who have similar reading levels and interests, and encouraging students to try out key academic terms in their focused talk as they answer questions they pose to each other. Each partner reads a page or section orally and then asks a question of the listener partner; partners then talk about the text.

Co-teachers can also support ELL students' learning of academic content by providing opportunities for them to talk and use academic vocabulary and discourse to make the concepts their own and to internalize the new ways of expressing ideas (Echevarria, Vogt, & Short, 2004; Marzano, 2004; Shanahan & Beck, 2007). However, before expecting ELL students to talk about academic content, co-teachers may need to ask the following questions:

- What are the incoming students' levels of proficiency and do they have enough understanding of the syntax of the English language to extend their discourse?
- What kinds of prior experiences do the students have in reading informational texts and asking and answering discussion questions?
- How can teachers use their students' background knowledge and reading experience when pairing them?

The PRC2 includes the stages described below. The description of each stage also includes various co-teaching examples to show how co-teaching can support both reading and speaking:

1. getting comfortable with text structure,
2. modeling partner routine and discussion routine,
3. asking and answering questions,
4. reading and discussing content,
5. scaffolding academic talk, and
6. whole-class discussion.

1. Getting Comfortable with Text Structure

If ELL students are to progress in content knowledge in the language domain of speaking, the level of reading materials needs to be at an appropriate reading fluency level "so students [can] focus on the content and develop vocabulary without being overwhelmed" (Ogle & Correa-Kovtun, 2010). Furthermore, "classrooms need to make available materials at a range of reading levels in the content being studied" (Allington, 2007; Allington & Cunningham, 2007).

Finally, students need "enough time to read and reread the texts carefully and to talk in a safe environment, with their partner about the ideas" (Ogle & Correa-Kovtun, 2010). When ELL students are paired according to similar reading levels and the focus is on content learning, they "try out the key academic terms and use them in their focused talk as they answer the questions they pose to each other" (2010).

One way co-teachers can support this stage is by using narrative text structure to assist reading comprehension. There are many ways to co-teach reading-comprehension skills that are not exclusive to expository texts such as the content areas of math and science. Students understand scientific content better when they can present it in more than one mode (Prain & Waldrip, 2006).

As Mills (2009) states, "Teachers should use authentic texts that are used in the world outside of school, highlighting their typical and atypical organizational features." Because students encounter multiple representations of content in school and an ever-increasing range of textual forms outside of school, collaboration of teachers across content areas can support students in understanding, critiquing, and designing a variety of texts.

For example, Mills (2009–2010) suggests using Pick-a-Plot, which focuses on narrative text structure and can assist reading comprehension across content areas. In small groups, students recreate and tell an original story by accessing information from either multi-modal texts (i.e., texts that convey meaning through multiple sign systems such as gestures, spoken words, written words, numeric equations, photographs, diagrams, and so forth) or new text forms. To this end, co-teachers can model the following according to the roles dictated by corresponding models:

Both teachers are directing the class and are in front of the class.

- On the level of story and vocabulary
  - The core-teacher introduces a particular text-type and discusses its structure and unique features.
  - The ESL teacher provides examples of the characters and the setting and clarifies key vocabulary. There are many "story" books that focus on science areas and themes like *The Magic School Bus* (Scholastic). Later, the teachers can "recycle" key vocabulary by distributing cards that provide suggestions for possible settings that are also based on previously introduced vocabulary words.
- On the level of reading comprehension
  - The core teacher pre-teaches the narrative structures of *plot*, *climax*, and *resolution* while the ESL teacher pre-teaches relevant vocabulary and provides specific examples for each one.

Activating Prior Knowledge of Multimodal Texts

Activating prior knowledge has an important role in the reading-comprehension process and especially with multimodal texts. If ELL students are to improve the way they access content and language, co-teachers can influence the way they help elicit background knowledge. As Mills states, "A stimulating repertoire of before reading speaking and listening activities can help students draw upon relevant cultural and language resources to make meaning and improve all levels of comprehension, from recall to inferential and critical thinking" (Anstey & Freebody, 1987).

Mills (2009–2010) gives the example of pretending to interview Barak Obama by having the students perform the interviews to a live audience or digitally recording the interview using a computer, microphone, and a simple sound-recording program. In this way, students are using real-world skills and authentic texts, and teachers are also appealing to various learning styles. If teachers find that their ELL students struggle with this task, they may need to pre-teach parts of it or delegate tasks to the more independent and advanced readers.

As students learn different genres in a variety of multimodal forms and representations on computer, television, and cell phone screens, eliciting what students know using hands-on approaches, particularly with abstract math and science concepts, is central to the students' learning about content areas.

2. Modeling Partner Routine and Discussion Routine

As a first step, co-teachers model targeted academic words so students have a better understanding of how to pronounce them before engaging in partner reading and discussion. (stages 4 and 6). Models such as turn-taking and direct teaching allow for some teacher exchange and exchange in pre-teaching content and academic vocabulary, which is suitable for setting up the PCR2 routine. "As the teachers model the partner reading process-by first reading both pages silently and then rereading their individual page to prepare for oral reading, they also model noticing unfamiliar words and figure out how to pronounce them" (Ogle & Correa-Kovtun, 2010).

One type of partner routine is paired reading to help ELL students engage in vocabulary practice. An example of paired reading follows:

- Speaking partner A reads the first sentence. Listening partner B helps.
- Speaking partner B reads the next sentence.
- Listening partner A helps.
- Then both partners "put their heads together" and summarize what they have read. They should be encouraged to use as many of the key words and concepts they have learned as possible. (Calderon, 2011, webinar)

3. Asking and Answering Questions

The use of questions promotes both language and content objectives, explores the relationships between questions and hierarchical thinking, and demonstrates effective questioning techniques. Skilled question use enhances meaningful communication, engagement, and understanding.

If co-teachers want their ELL students to develop higher-level thinking, they need to pre-teach strategies to help show ELL students how to develop opinions of what they read. Both teachers, for example, can model how to read important information as well as ask the questions "What have I missed?" and "What is my opinion of the issue?" (Mills, 2009; 2010).

Co-teachers can also model "ways of talking about student-generated questions and analyze good questions" (Ogle & Correa-Kovtun, 2010) that reinforce how to think about what ELL students are reading if they are to be actively engaged and stimulated when discussing academic content. Bloom's Taxonomy, for example, provides a hierarchy of thinking skills that guides teaching. In a collaborative framework, for example, both teachers would be responsible for encouraging and stimulating deeper thinking about specific words and their concepts as illustrated in the examples below:

- Tell: how, when, where, why
- Tell: what would happen
- Tell: how much change would there be.

Alternatively, as explained by Ogle & Correa-Kovtun (2010), teachers can provide a question matrix with four questions:

1. What was most important? Why? Explain.
2. What was most interesting? Why? Explain.
3. What connections can you make? Explain.
4. What could the author make clearer? Explain.

Collaboration in Action

One possible configuration is for either the ESL or content-area teacher to work with two separate groups. With one group, one teacher provides questions that encourage and stimulate deeper thinking on especially difficult academic concepts and terms while the other teacher circulates around the classroom helping individual pairs in their academic discussions.

When discussing the science concepts of heat, energy, force, or work in science, for example, teachers can use Bloom's Taxonomy to help teach students about how to address these concepts as *processes*, as when teachers say: "Tell me how block and tackle work or how a second or third class level works." Teachers would elicit specific relevant vocabulary and draw visuals to aid in understanding.

Another configuration includes the following:

Table 2.1

ESL Teacher	Content-Area Teacher
Depending on the role of L1, the ESL teacher may demonstrate this process in L1. Alternatively, the ESL teacher can also provide examples and use visuals such as flash cards or the smartboard to highlight WH question words or to pre-teach the order of questions.	The content-area teacher models how to read for important information for specific purposes. S/he also explains that questions have different depths, contrasting questions that require information recall with those that require drawing inferences (Mills, 2009–2010).

4. Reading and Discussing Content

Co-teachers can provide opportunities for ELL students to own more of the academic vocabulary and content concepts by helping ELL students use them in their talk. To minimize teacher talk, co-teachers can discuss how to give students enough time to practice text reading and talk using the key vocabulary without co-teachers doing all of the oral presentation. Pair work helps ELL students practice using important academic vocabulary. If teachers want to promote more classroom interaction, pairing students with similar reading and language development will also help both students feel comfortable participating in the ongoing exchanges (Ogle & Correa-Kovtun, 2010).

5. Scaffolding Academic Talk

A big part of scaffolding academic talk has to do with bridging content with background knowledge in terms of what students know. For example, when getting students to see different word meanings in both everyday speech and content areas such as *force* and *work*, one way is to have students think and map word meanings. For example, a co-teacher teachers can model, "Let's map out 'work' as in the sentence 'I worked really hard on this project.'" In science, however, the meaning of *work* is "energy," and together with the co-teacher, students can draw a little picture of what *work* looks like in science.

Similarly, with the everyday use of the word *force*, a co-teacher can say, "Your mother forces you to do the dishes," or, "May the force be with you," and then use graphic organizers, charts, and tables to explain the science-based meaning.

6. Whole-Class Discussion

In preparing students to discuss specific vocabulary, teachers can provide a list of vocabulary words whereby students begin to categorize them in the following K-W-L chart:

Table 2.2

Know	Familiar	Need to Know
I know this word and can use it in a sentence. I can explain it to another person.	I have heard this word before, but I cannot use it or define it.	I have never heard this word before.

Co-teachers can then discuss various vocabulary (depending on the content area) either in isolation or in context using one of the various models described in chapter 1.

Best Practices in the Classroom

When getting her students to talk about precise science definitions, Kelly Grucelski asks her fifth-grade ELL students to take out their notesheets. For example, when students are recalling the subject of simple machines, they look at their notesheets, which consist of a definition for each machine and a picture. By having them take notes, they become more independent in their work habits and develop academic vocabulary awareness. A student sample follows:

Simple Machines Vocabulary

Word	It can mean...	but in SCIENCE it means...	Picture
Force	Air force, forced, forcing, you to do, forceful, homework, did away, the force may be with you	is a push or pull on an object	
Machine	Soda machine, vending machine, sewing machine, washing machine, icecream machine	an object that makes work easier	
Simple	Plain, easy math, simple water, simple homework, simple machine	uncomplicated, one or two parts	
Work	mathwork, laundry, classwork, workout	when an object moves due to a force working upon it $W = F \times D$	

PROMOTING CLASSROOM INTERACTION IN VERY YOUNG ELL STUDENTS (UNDER 7) AND YOUNG ELL STUDENTS (7–12)

Developing speaking requires a great deal of teacher modeling and opportunities for classroom interaction specifically between ELL students and their native English-speaking peers. If ELL students are to feel confident when interacting in class, co-teachers need to create a nonthreatening classroom environment.

Young English language learners (7–12) are developing as thinkers and can work with others and learn from others, while English language learners under the age of seven acquire language through hearing and experiencing lots of English, in much the same way they acquire L1. Their grammar will also develop gradually on its own when they are exposed to lots of English in context (Slattery & Willis, 2001).

Even though very young ELL students are not able to organize their learning, they can still participate and cooperate in classroom activities and interact during class. All learners can take a risk while making mistakes where they try out, experiment, and create with the language. They will also need to consider the role of L1 in the language-learning environment if ELL students are to acquire a second language effectively. In the L1 environment of English language learning, language is highly contextualized, and in the real world, the language used is authentic. Therefore, it is very important for co-teachers to provide authentic language situations.

It's crucial to teach young ELL students academic content before they are expected to demonstrate greater understanding of content-specific texts. However, co-teachers have to make sure they are incorporating speaking effectively as illustrated in the following co-teaching lesson-planning form.

Name of co-teachers: _____
Name of content area unit: _____
Grade: _____
Week of: _____
Type of model: _____
Activities to develop speaking and vocabulary:
_____
_____
_____

Targeted vocabulary: _____
Collaborative model: _____

PREPARATION FOR TESOL/WIDA STANDARDS

Prior to planning and implementing EL science instruction in a co-teaching framework, teachers need profiles of students and language demands. In science inquiry activities, for example, ELL students are expected to do the following activities listed below regularly. Before matching English language proficiency standards to language demands, co-teachers will need to analyze the language demands of the content topic. For example, in an inquiry-based science classroom, ELL students will need to do the following on a regular basis:

- read and follow instruction on data sheets;
- listen to, understand, and interpret information given orally;
- participate in cooperative learning groups in which information is shared;
- speak to explain their point of view; and
- write journal entries, reports, and narratives related to their science investigations. (Thier, 2002)

Since the movement of energy and how it transforms is a difficult concept for ELL students to grasp, co-teachers can offer students the opportunity to understand and reflect on abstract concepts by providing instructional strategies such as direct instruction and inquiry. Co-teaching plays an important role in planning, presenting, and assessing thematic inquiry-based science lessons for ELL students in multi-level classes. Below, teachers will find sample co-teaching objectives that have been adapted from the energy unit listed by the Pennsylvania Department of Education.

Sample co-teaching objectives and activities in light of energy unit:

- To *parallel teach* in the content area of science, by addressing the same standards, key vocabulary, and reading and writing skills, and by building background knowledge and reviewing key concepts and language structures.
- To provide *direct instruction* to help students understand simple concepts of how energy moves and transforms using the following *suggested models*: both teachers are directing the class and in front of the class, turn-taking, role-switching, and parallel teaching.
- To provide *direct instruction* that also grabs students' interest and provides several hands-on activities that anchor students' understanding of abstract concepts about energy. *Suggested models*: directing the class and in front of the class, turn-taking, and role switching. Parallel teaching is also an option.
- To demonstrate how one source of energy or object can move another object and transfer the energy using hands-on activities (see sample activities below) that are also based on authentic learning (real-world experiences) that helps co-teachers also extend the learning from their background information.
- To combine the skills of writing for understanding the energy concepts and reading for meaning.
- To pace instruction by presenting scientific concepts and content-specific vocabulary, and, finally, to help ELL students ask and answer questions as one way to strengthen the process of scientific inquiry and develop their confidence in speaking about difference types of energy.

USING A TURN-TAKING MODEL TO TEACH VOCABULARY

The following scenario shows a turn-taking model in action with a modified script that supports explicit vocabulary instruction. In this sample scenario, the ESL teacher pre-teaches vocabulary while the core teacher presents the concepts. Before engaging students in reading a text, the ESL teacher can use a large number of photos or realia including tangible and concrete objects like images, pictures, and hand movements and gestures to help negotiate meaning of the target word—for example, *crust*—and connect vocabulary to concrete objects and body language to act out specific concepts, and colorful highlighters to mark keywords.

Visual methods are important for supporting meaning and generating interest, especially with abstract concepts of scientific language, and so are activities—such as group work—that allow students "to try on new words and get a feel for them promote student competency in talking, thinking, and inquiring like a scientist" (Ciechanowski, 2009).

ESL teacher: So, let's think of the ways you might hear *crust* in a different context like "I ate all the pie for Thanksgiving including the crust." How are these meanings different? (Here, she offers exposure to a word in multiple forms.)

As a follow-up, the ESL teacher can also elicit from the students both student-friendly and formal definitions or can offer them without eliciting from the students. She can highlight characteristics or word parts in *crust* such as pronunciation. The ESL teacher can also act as a teacher modeler by first pointing to the word *crust* and asking the core teacher, "How do you pronounce *crust*?" The core teacher can respond with "It's *crust*" (with accent on the first syllable).

Questions for co-teachers:

- Which model will help teach vocabulary, reading-comprehension skills, and writing that are specific to a content area?
- What kind of opportunities can co-teachers offer for developing the language domain of speaking in the content area of science? As Lemke (1990) states, "Students should regularly have oral, and occasionally written, practice in class in restating scientific expressions in their own colloquial words, and also in translating colloquial arguments into formal scientific language" (p.173).

On the level of vocabulary, the ESL teacher can discuss phrasal words in context such as *pass on energy* and elicit other word meanings such as *transfer* and elicit background knowledge of *energy transfer* to cement the linguistic understanding. At the level of understanding the abstract concept of *passing on energy*, co-teachers can reinforce the concept that energy is transferred or moved from one object or place to another—that energy is not something one can see or hear, but it is a state of ongoing motion. Finally, co-teachers can also discuss the meanings of *energy* as ELL students might hear them in other contexts.

MATCHING ENGLISH LANGUAGE PROFICIENCY STANDARDS TO LANGUAGE DEMANDS

Once co-teachers determine English language learners' current language profiles and analyze the language demands of the content topic, they can match English language proficiency (ELP) standards to language demands.

Differentiate Activities According to Language of Proficiency

One way teachers can ensure they are meeting the academic and language needs of their ELL students is by differentiating instruction. Research suggests that instruction that integrates science and language-development objectives and

Table 2.3. Sample Science and Language Standards for Energy in Motion

Science Standards Science Content Standards for Pennsylvania Public Schools, Grade 4 (Pennsylvania Department of Education, 2010)		
Science Academic Skills Students have the necessary academic abilities to conduct a scientific investigation	Science Content Standards *Energy in Motion* 1. All types of energy can be stored and changed from one form to another.	*Forms, Sources, Conversion, and Transfer of Energy* 2. The flow of energy appears through all kinds of energy forms, transfer, and examples such as light, heat, and electrical.

Sample from TESOL Standard 4 English Language Standards PreK–12 English Language Proficiency Standards (TESOL, 2006)	
English language learners **communicate** information, ideas, and concepts necessary for academic success in the area of science.	
Grade Level 4–5	*Level 5*
Speaking (earth's materials, natural resources)	Explain relationships among natural phenomena using extended discourse

experiences can meet the unique needs of ELL students (Echevarria, Vogt, & Short, 2008). For example, teachers can offer varied choices and alternatives for those students who are struggling to understand science concepts and inquiry.

Some ELL students might be better readers while others may not have a lot of background knowledge. In this way, co-teachers can help those who are not at the same starting place. For example, to suit a co-teaching context, co-teachers can form two groups and adjust the task so that the advanced group discusses the meanings of *energy* as students might hear them in other contexts using target vocabulary words, and the less advanced group focuses on a specific number of words.

Best Practices in the Classroom

At Sagamore Middle School at Sachem Central School District in New York, one of the ESL teachers, Aristea Lucas, who had successfully taught K–6 ESL pull-out and push-in programs, was asked to help implement a collaborative ESL program at the middle-school level for grades 6–8 in the year 2010 as a three-year pilot. Sagamore Middle School is one of those schools that has collaborative school structures in place by way of shared decision-making for curriculum and instruction for ELL students. There are three full-time ESL teachers who also co-teach with content-area teachers. All teachers have co-taught in history, science, math, and ELA. Below are two observation snippets of math and science co-lessons.

Sixth-Grade Science

During a sixth-grade science class, students are instructed to use the periodic table to find protons, neutrons, and electrons. In this reading-comprehension lesson, one student reads aloud while the content-area teacher explains how to find the atomic mass and the mass number of an atom. Some key terms and terminology such as *atomic mass, total mass of the protons and neutrons in an atom*, and *measured in atomic mass units* (amu) appear on an overhead transparency.

Through a modeling process of questions and answers, the content-area teacher extends the modeling process and calls several students to share their answers mostly to inference-type questions. Gathered around the desk is a group of ELL students, including a new ELL student. Prior to the lesson, the small group of ELL students was taught to define the parts of the atom vocabulary orally and in writing and to identify the parts of an atom. Targeted vocabulary included: nucleus, atoms, protons, electrons, neutrons, and neutral.

While the content-area teacher talks, the ESL teacher works with the small group of ELL students answering questions and clarifying information while they are learning the same content. To complete the three worksheets, students needed to know how to use the periodic table and the atomic number and atomic mass. The texts themselves are dense, scattered with targeted vocabulary in varied contexts. When a native English-speaking peer gets up, one of the ELL students raises his hand to volunteer his answer. As he completes one of the elements in the periodic table using knowledge of atoms and the periodic table, the rest of the class claps joyously.

Sixth-Grade Math Lesson

During a parallel teaching lesson of twenty-seven students with five English language learners, both co-teachers address key concepts and vocabulary mainly by using proportions to figure out distances from one area of the map to the other. Both co-teachers manage classroom routines by taking attendance, distributing materials, giving instruction, and keeping discipline.

When it comes to direct instruction and presenting information in sequence, each follows a slightly different routine. One uses the smartboard while the other uses a document camera and both model problem-solving strategies as well as monitor and check students' understanding of the rules of proportion directly in front of the class. They emphasize target terminology through the use of direct closed and open types of questions to draw student interest and establish the topic. For example: What's another word for =? What is an atlas? Who uses it? Can we use an atlas instead of a GPS?

For the main bulk of the lesson, the students are engaged in practice-type questions where students need to calculate how to get from New York to California. Both teachers model instruction by helping students set up a ratio while the co-teachers mark the places on the board and use a scale to mark the places.

Fifth-Grade Math

Kelly Grucelski, a fifth-grade ELL teacher at the Partnership Academy, uses a "Greater Common Factor" and the "Least Common Multiple" graphic organizers to anchor her ELL students' understanding of math concepts. As a class, they fill in the chart together and then ELL students use their own version as a reference to check how they are reducing/simplifying, adding, subtracting, or comparing fractions.

Best Practices in the Content-Area Classrooms

At a middle school in Queens, there is a constant push for integrating content in the ESL classrooms. Cindy Kontente, an ESL teacher, felt fortunate that her administration supported co-teaching. However, she was cognizant of the limited amount of time teachers had to engage in this work. She believed content teachers and ESL teachers would be more receptive to co-teaching if there were more time built into their weekly schedules.

Because teachers constantly came to her for advice, help, and support, she realized how "hungry" they were for ongoing ELL professional development. In 2007, she conducted workshops for an Ex-CELL professional-development program. The strategies presented were initially designed for ELLs, but have proven effective for all students.

When Cindy became a high school ESL teacher at the Queens High School of Teaching, one of her many roles was to visit grade team meetings to discuss the ELLs on Student Talk days. She spoke with all of the content-area teachers and gave them suggestions, tips, and strategies to support the ELLs in their classrooms. But she was always well aware that more could and should be done to support the ELLs. A major issue in high schools across the country is the high dropout rate or low graduation rate of ELLs.

Now, as an assistant principal at the Queens High School of Teaching, Ms. Kontente spends a significant amount of time training content-area teachers to implement strategies in their classrooms to serve the needs of all of the students, including ELLs and students who receive accommodations. She says, "As a school leader in an inclusion high school in Queens, I am committed to improving instruction to increase student achievement and learning. I am focused on supporting teachers to scaffold their instruction to meet the needs of all of our students to ensure an optimal level of success."

Cindy Kontente and Ean Corrado, another assistant principal at the Queens High School of Teaching, created a "Co-Teaching Unit/Lesson Planning Template." This has been implemented in the Montessori Small Learning Community at the school to guarantee best-practice instruction.

Co-teaching Discussions in Content Areas

Incorporating visuals and manipulatives and reading word problems aloud is not enough to address the needs of ELL students. By helping ELL students learn key strategies, they can succeed in learning mathematical concepts and, simultaneously, learn English. For this reason, Kelly Grucelski and her co-teacher created a graphic organizer designed to cement conceptual understanding with greatest common factor (GCF) and least common multiple (LCM).

Both Kelly Grucelski and her co-teacher anticipated that their students would mix up the processes of finding the GCF and LCM since they work with less-advanced students who are also at a high-intermediate/low-advanced level of English. As a result of their co-planning conversation, Ms. Grucelski suggested creating a graphic organizer, or an anchor chart that would hang in the classroom where both co-teachers could read it during direct instruction and for students to work independently while solving math problems. Now when they co-teach students how to reduce fractions and compare fractions, they always refer back to the anchor chart and ask them to pull out their own versions to remind themselves how to find the GCF or LCM.

Table 2.4. Montessori SLC Co-teaching Unit/Lesson-Planning Template (Three Class Periods)

The following document is intended to provide support and scaffolding to co-teachers during weekly co-planning/lesson-preparation meetings. By engaging in professional dialogue and completing the document, co-teachers will create a collaborative plan for a week of classroom instruction. Used effectively, the Montessori SLC Co-teaching Unit/Lesson-Planning Template will guide both the processes and the products of a successful co-teaching relationship and will support the creation of best-practice learning experiences for our students.

During co-teaching planning sessions, for their own records (both in preparation for and during the facilitation of classes), both teachers should complete a copy of the template. Additionally, during the facilitation of the classes outlined below, the completed template can be referred to and used to guide instruction. Lesson plans will supplement the work outlined below and should be shared and retained by both teachers to ensure continuity of best-practice instruction in the event of teacher absence.

Teachers:		Subject Area:
Week of:	Theme/Topic:	Essential Question(s):

Class Period 1	Feedback Strategies for Differentiation/Modifications
Focus Question:	
Warm-up:	
Learning Goal(s):	
Checks(s) for Understanding:	
Day's Agenda	

(continued)

Table 2.4. *(Continued)*

Co-teaching Approaches	
One Teach, One Observe ☐	
Station Teaching ☐	Alternative Teaching ☐
One Lead, One Support ☐	Teaming ☐

Class Period 2	Feedback Strategies for Differentiation/Modifications
Focus Question:	
Warm-up:	
Learning Goal(s):	
Check(s) for Understanding:	
Day's Agenda	
Co-teaching Approaches	
One Lead, One Support ☐	
Station Teaching ☐	Alternative Teaching ☐
Parallel Teaching ☐	Team Teaching ☐

Class Period 3	Feedback Strategies for Differentiation Modifications
Focus Question:	
Warm-up:	
Learning Goal(s):	
Check(s) for Understanding:	
Day's Agenda	
Co-teaching Approaches	

One Lead, One Support ☐	
Stations Teaching ☐	Alternative Teaching ☐
Parallel Teaching ☐	Teaming ☐

| thousandth | seven |

G.C.F	L.C.M
Stands for: Greatest Common Factor	Stands for: Least Common Multiple
Example: 12 and 6 6: <u>1, 2, 3, 6</u> 12: <u>1, 2, 3,</u> 4, <u>6,</u> 12 Least ———→ Greatest GCF = 6	Example: 5 and 6 5: 5, 10, 15, 20, 25, ㉚ 6: 6, 12, 18, 24, ㉚ LCM = 30
When we use it: • Reduce Fractions • Simplify Fractions	When we use it: • Add Fractions • Subtract Fractions • Compare Fractions

G.C.F.	L.C.M.
Stands for: Greatest Common Factor	Stands for: Least Common Multiple
Example: 12 and 6 — Least to Greatest 6: 6, 12 12: 12, 24... GCF = 6	Example: 5 and 6 (M diagram) LCM = 30
When we use it: • Reduce fractions • Simplify fractions	When we use it: • When we add fractions • When we subtract fractions • Compare fractions

CHAPTER SUMMARY

Providing opportunities for ELL students to talk about academic texts is an ongoing challenge for co-teachers as well as for ELL students. Through constant planning and instruction, co-teachers need to ensure they are fostering the use of teaching and learning strategies to help make academic material comprehensible for ELL students on both speaking and reading levels. This ongoing work also requires that ESL teachers be knowledgeable of the content areas such as math and science while content-area teachers who are trained in second-language acquisition and language teaching strategies can establish access to the core curriculum for ELL students.

By using conversational and oral reading strategies, co-teachers can also pre-teach academic and subject-specific vocabulary with a cross-disciplinary focus that helps ELL students think and talk about content-area concepts, ask and answer questions, and discuss related themes and concepts.

FURTHER READING

Oral Language Assessment Tools

O'Malley, J. M., & Pierce, L. V. (1996). *Authentic assessment for English language learners: Practical approaches for teachers.* Reading, MA: Addison-Wesley. (An important resource that helps with developing "mini-assessments" and helps keep ELL students on track.)

Pierce, L. V. (2003). *Assessing English language learners.* Washington, DC: National Education Association.

Resources on Science and Academic Language

Rosebery, A. S., & Warren, B. (Eds.). (2008). *Teaching science to English language learners: Building on students' strengths.* Arlington, VA: National Science Teachers Association.

Zwiers, J. (2008). *Building academic language: Essential practices for content classrooms.* San Francisco: Jossey-Bass.

ACTIVITIES FOR FURTHER COLLABORATION

1. In teacher teams, try out an activity described in this chapter. What worked? What didn't? What's next?
2. Using a reflection journal, make notes for the following areas over the course of a week:

	Types of speaking activities/ strategies each teacher used. What was the purpose?	How did our speaking activities/ strategies support the phases of reading and vocabulary instruction across content areas?	What did each teacher do at each stage of our reading instruction?
Lesson one, week one			
Lesson two, week one			
Lesson three, week one			
Lesson four, week one			
Lesson five, week one			

With a co-teacher, discuss how you were able to coordinate and maximize your roles using the collaborative model for the sake of supporting ELL students in the area of speaking across content areas. Were you able to coordinate speaking activities and apply them to the phases of before, during, and after reading instruction? What worked? What didn't? What's next?

QUESTIONS FOR DISCUSSION

1. How can co-teaching be used to increase vocabulary progress in the language domain of speaking?
2. With either a partner or teams, identify some of the challenges in increasing students' oral English production in terms of the quantity and quality of interaction in the classroom. How can co-teaching effectively address some of these challenges?

REFERENCES

Adams, M. J. (1990). *Beginning to read: Thinking and learning about print*. Cambridge: MIT Press.

Allington, R. L. (2007). Intervention all day long: New hope for struggling readers. *Voices from the Middle, 14*(4), 7–14.

Allington, R. L., & Cunningham, P. M. (2007). *Schools that work: Where all children read and write* (3rd ed.). Boston: Pearson.

Almasi, J. F. (1996). A new view of discussion. In L. B. Gambrell & J. F. Almasi (Eds.), *Lively discussions! Fostering engaged reading* (pp. 2–24). Newark, DE: International Reading Association.

Anstey, M., & Bull, G. (2004). *The literacy labyrinth* (2nd ed.). Frenchs Forest, NSW: Pearson.

Anstey, M., & Freebody, P. (1987). The effects of various prereading activities on children's literal and inferential comprehension. *Reading Psychology, 8*(3), 189–209. doi:10.1080/0270271870080305

August, D., Carlo, M. S., Dressler, C., & Snow, C. E. (2005). The critical role of vocabulary development for English language learners. *Learning Disabilities Research & Practice, 20*(1), 50–57. doi: 10.1111/j.1540-5826.2005.00120x

Ballard, R. D. (1993). *Finding the Titanic*. New York: Scholastic.

Brumfit, C. (1984). *Communicative methodology in language teaching: The roles of fluency and accuracy.* Cambridge: Cambridge University Press.

Bybee, R., Taylor, J. A., Gardner, A., Van Scotter, P., Carlson, J., Westbrook, A., & Landes, N. (2006). *The BSCS 5E instructional model: Origins and effectiveness.* Colorado Springs: BSCS.

Ciechanowski, K. M. (2009). "A squirrel came and pushed earth": Popular cultural and scientific ways of thinking for ELLs. *The Reading Teacher, 62*(7), 558–568. doi: 10.1598/RT.62.7.2

Cullinan, B. E. (Ed.). (1993). *Children's voices: Talk in the classroom*. Newark, DE: International Reading Association.

Cummins, J., & Swain, M. (1986). *Bilingualism in education: Aspects of theory, research, and practice*. New York: Longman.

Cunningham, P., & Allington, R. (2007) Classrooms that work: They can all read and write (5th ed.). Boston: Pearson Education.

Cramer, R. L. (2004). *The language arts: A balanced approach to teaching reading, writing, listening, talking, and thinking*. New York: Pearson Education.

Dickinson, D. K., & Smith, M. W. (1994). Long-term effects of pre-school teachers' book readings on low-income children's vocabulary and story comprehension. *Reading Research Quarterly, 29*(2), 104–122. doi: 10.2307/747807

Echevarria, J., Vogt, M. E., & Short, D. (2004). *Making content comprehensible for English learners: The SIOP model* (2nd ed.). Boston: Pearson Education.

Ellis, R. (1994). *Second language acquisition*. Oxford: Oxford University Press.

Fish, S. (1980). *Is there a text in this class: The authority of interpretive communities*. Cambridge: Harvard University Press.

Fitzgerald, J., Amendum, S. J., & Guthrie, K. M. (2008). Young Latino students' English-reading growth in all-English classrooms. *Journal of Literacy Research, 40*(1), 59–94. doi:10.1080/10862960802070459

Gottlieb, M., Katz, A., & Ernst-Slavik, G. (2006). *Paper to practice: Using the TESOL English language proficiency standards in preK–12 classrooms*. Alexandria, VA: TESOL.

Hampton, S., & Resnick, L. B. (2009). *Reading and writing with understanding: Comprehension in fourth and fifth grades*. Newark, DE: International Reading Association.

Harmer, J. (2011, November 16). The Fluency Paradox Revisited. TESOL Virtual Seminar.
Jenkins, J. (2006), Points of view and blind spots: ELF and SLA. *International Journal of Applied Linguistics, 16*, 137–162. doi: 10.1111/j.1473-4192.2006.00111.x
Lemke, J. L. (1990). *Talking science: Language, learning, and values*. Norwood, NJ: Ablex.
Lesaux, N., & Geva, E. (2006). Synthesis: Development of literacy in language-minority students. In D. August & T. Shanahan (Eds.), *Developing literacy in second-language learners: Report of the national literacy panel on language-minority children and youth* (pp. 53–74). Mahwah, NJ: Erlbaum.
MacDonald, C., & Figueredo, L. (2010). Closing the gap early: Implementing a literacy intervention for at-risk kindergartners in urban schools. *The Reading Teacher, 63*(5), 404–419. doi:10.1598/RT.63.5.6
Marzano, R. J. (2004). *Building background knowledge for academic achievement: Research on what works in schools*. Alexandria, VA: Association for Supervision and Curriculum Development.
Mills, K. A. (2009–2010). Floating on a sea of talk: Reading comprehension through speaking and listening. *Reading Teacher, 63*(4), 325–329. doi: 10.1598?RT.63.4.8
Mora, J. K. (2009). From the ballot box to the classroom. *Educational Leadership, 66*(7), 14–19.
Morris, D., Bloodgood, J., & Perney, J. (2003). Kindergarten predictors of first- and second-grade reading achievement. *The Elementary School Journal, 104*(2), 93–109. doi: 10.1086/499744
Morrison, V., & Wlodarczyk, L. (2009). Revisiting read-aloud: Instructional strategies that encourage students' engagement with texts. *The Reading Teacher, 63*(2), 110–118. doi: 10.1598/RT.63.2.2
Nation, K., & Snowling, M. J. (2004). Beyond phonological skills: Broader language skills contribute to the development of reading. *Journal of Research in Reading, 27*(4), 342–356. doi:10.1111/j.1467-9817.2004.00238x
Ogle, D., & Correa-Kovtun, A. (2010). Supporting English-language learners and struggling readers in content literacy with the "partner reading and content, too" routine. *The Reading Teacher, 63*(7), 532–542. doi: 10.1598/RT.63.7.1
Prain, V., & Waldrip, B. (2006). An exploratory study of teachers' and students' use of multimodal representations of concepts in primary science. *International Journal of Science Education, 28*(15), 1843–1866. doi: 10.1080/09500690600718294
Pullen, P. C., & Justice, L. M. (2003). Enhancing phonological awareness, print awareness, and oral language skills in preschool children. *Intervention in School and Clinic, 39*(2), 87–98. doi:10.1177/10534512030390020401
Shanahan, T., & Beck, I. L. (2006). Effective literacy teaching for English-language learners. In D. August & T. Shanahan (Eds.), *Developing literacy in second-language learners: Report of the National Literacy Panel on language-minority children and youth* (pp. 415–488). Mahwah, NJ: Erlbaum.
Slattery, M., & Willis, J. (2001). *English for primary teachers*. Oxford: Oxford University Press.
Snow, C. E., Burns, M. S., & Griffin, P. (Eds.). (1998). *Preventing reading difficulties in young children*. Washington, DC: National Academy Press.

Stahl, S. A. (2001). Teaching phonics and phonological awareness. In S. B. Neuman & D. K. Dickinson (Eds.), *Handbook of early literacy research* (vol. 1, pp. 333–347). New York: Guildford.

Stierer, B., & Maybin, J. (1994). *Language, literacy, and learning in educational practice*. Clevedon, England: Multilingual Matters.

Thier, Marlene. (2002). *The new science literacy: Using language skills to help students learn science*. Portsmouth, NH: Heinemann.

Trehearne, M. (2000). *Kindergarten teacher's resource book*. Scarborough, ON, Canada: Nelson Education.

Wasik, B. A. (2010). What teachers can do to promote preschoolers' vocabulary development: Strategies from an effective language and literacy professional development coaching model. *The Reading Teacher, 63*(8), 621–633. doi: 10.1598/RT.63.8.1h

Whitehurst, G. J., Falco, F. L., Lonigan, C. J., Fischel, J. E., DeBaryshe, B. D., Valdez-Menchaca, M. C., & Caulfield, M. (1988). Accelerating language development through picture book reading. *Developmental Psychology, 24*(4), 552–559. doi: 10.1037/00121649.24.4.552

Wolf, M. K., Crosson, A. C., & Resnick, L. B. (2004). Classroom talk for rigorous reading comprehension instruction. *Reading Psychology, 26*(1), 27–53. doi:10.1080/02702710490897518

Wong Fillmore, L., & Snow, C. E. (2000). *What teachers need to know about language*. Washington, DC: Center for Applied Linguistics.

Chapter Three

Collaboration in the Development of Writing Skills

Writing is often viewed by teachers as an important skill that has to be catered for and developed for ELL students. Engaging students in written communication in a variety of forms connects learners to the international world of information in every field via electronic communication such as Internet and personal correspondence across the border. Many English language learners have strong oral abilities but lack confidence in their writing skills. As a result, many resist taking risks in their writing and teachers often find their writing difficult to read and overcorrect their mistakes.

Teachers are sensitive to the diverse backgrounds that define their students, but because students often do not feel comfortable expressing themselves in writing and especially in a second language, this often complicates teaching and assessment. To address this issue, teachers can provide meaningful academic and nonacademic activities to connect ELL students to the classroom experience. Meaningful writing activities tie both motivation and ability and encourage a variety of expressions that do not limit a student's language ability. The student's ability to write about topics that are close to a student's culture, experiences, and other topics of interest increases when one also feels more connected with learning the target language.

This chapter explores the complexities of writing for K–6 ELL students and provides clear guidance on how co-teachers can address and support these needs. This chapter begins by describing some of the co-teaching challenges and obstacles when supporting writing. Next, it defines *reluctant writers* and explains how teachers can scaffold and model writing instruction. It also considers some characteristics of how co-teachers can monitor areas of quality writing instruction and how ELL students acquire comprehension skills.

Questions this chapter will cover:

- What are some of the problems and challenges of teaching writing in today's elementary ELL general-education classrooms?
- How can teachers collaborate on vocabulary progress in the language domain of writing?
- How can teachers address reluctant writers and provide them with meaningful writing opportunities that also challenge them academically?
- How can co-teachers cater to the writing-development needs of K–2 students?
- How can teachers provide an effective framework for early elementary guided writing instruction that includes opportunities for reading and writing?

PROBLEMS AND CHALLENGES IN TEACHING WRITING IN TODAY'S ELEMENTARY ELL GENERAL-EDUCATION CLASSROOMS

The challenges of academically supporting ELL students in writing are common to many classrooms across the nation, and this testifies to the fact that ELL students cannot always do the same work as native English speakers without additional scaffolding of instruction and content. Acquiring reading and writing skills complicates the process for all ELL students and there are numerous opportunities to co-teach and collaborate by integrating a wide range of scaffoldings. At the middle-elementary level, teachers need to ensure they are teaching a balanced approach to writing that includes opportunities for reading and writing.

Background of English Language Learners

Because English language learners need to adjust to the cultural, linguistic, social, and emotional newness of a classroom environment, they may not have sufficient background knowledge to access academic vocabulary and content knowledge. As Spence states, "A student's culture, home language, history, and social settings are foundational to writing instruction and must be built upon before writing can be further assessed for competence" (2010).

Consequently, teachers' expectations, particularly around writing, need to be structured differently. Students from strong oral backgrounds tend to feel more comfortable expressing themselves orally in English and, as a result, they may show resistance to putting their thoughts on paper. They may also favor personal writing over expository writing and rely exclusively on their oral language because it requires less mental effort.

RATE OF ACADEMIC DEVELOPMENT VERSUS SOCIAL LANGUAGE

For ELL students, writing is where BICS (social language) and CALP (academic language) are demonstrated in the most formal and difficult mode of communication. Spolsky (1989), in his theory of second-language learning, imposes a set of conditions that shape acquisition. Among them is the recognition that individual language learners vary in their productive and receptive skills, with receptive language (listening and reading) generally developing prior to and at a higher level than productive language (speaking and writing). Thus, English language learners may not be at a uniform level of English language proficiency across the four domains.

This pattern may also be reflected in native-language proficiency. Unless English language learners have received formal instruction in their native language, their oral language or literacy may not be fully developed for their age level. The differential language acquisition of these students in the four language domains must be taken into consideration in instructional planning and assessment.

The emphasis in ELA literacy as part of the new Common Core State Standards is moving toward academic standards of written expression. In this new shift, students are expected to produce informational texts. To this end, teachers need to quickly provide the appropriate vocabulary and phrases students need to communicate their intended thoughts and ideas.

Even with teachers' steady preparation, many ELL students may not be ready to produce the appropriate level of output needed prior to production. ELL students may require additional scaffolding with reading texts before they are ready to produce the level of output that is comparable to that of national and state standards. Before middle-elementary ELL students can generate their own informational texts, they may also need practice developing prewriting tasks such as note-taking skills, paraphrasing, and sentence structure and form for longer, more rigorous writing tasks.

TEACHING CHALLENGES

Teaching and assessing writing become complicated due to the complex process by which ELL students acquire a second language. Depending on the context, teachers may find that the way their individual states mandate English instruction and the English writing rubric for annual assessments are problematic for the ELL students in their classrooms.

Teachers may feel compelled to search for a way to help ELL students become better writers despite their lower achievements. As ELL students acquire more English, teachers may need to constantly reexamine rubric descriptors in order to satisfy both reading and writing elements of language acquisition since writing is complex and recursive and, over time, all aspects of writing steadily improve.

Additionally, teachers may tend to think of mathematics as a subject that does not require a strong command of language. But, in fact, this is not the case. Mathematical reasoning and problem-solving are closely linked to language and rely upon a firm understanding of basic math vocabulary (Dale & Cuevas, 1992; Jarret, 1999). The challenge for teachers, of course, is to incorporate language-based instruction in academic and content-based learning.

The National Council of Teachers of Mathematics' (2000) *Principles and Standards for School Mathematics* now includes communication as a process strand. "Students need to be able to explain their problem solving methods orally and in written form, both in the classroom and on high-stakes tests" (Pierce & Fontaine, 2009). Using a comprehensive approach to bridge math and content, by "incorporating mathematics into a story and pictures . . . would help the reader think about mathematics in a new or deeper way" (Carter, 2009).

HOW COLLABORATION AND CO-TEACHING ADDRESS THESE ISSUES

Teaching Challenges

During their planning time, for example, co-teachers can conduct writing assessments. Spence (2010) suggests the occasional reading of students' writing (or in-depth of one student) in order to design instruction that builds upon students' strengths or to find ways to assess students' writing to determine the effect of a unit of study.

By reading students' writing, co-teachers can share writing samples and discuss insights of the lives, thoughts, and writing processes of students. Depending on the teaching topic and writing assignment, co-teachers can discuss the following elements in categories that both inform second-language acquisition and influence the way teachers co-teach and assess areas of writing and the writing process.

If writing from sources is to include more emphasis on building language, literacy, and content, teachers will need to rethink the reciprocal role of writing in reading-based lessons. In a collaborative context, therefore, ELL students will need to better understand content-rich expository and personal-narrative-type texts so they can respond to a sentence or paragraph prompt both orally and in writing.

Teachers cannot afford to wait until the beginning of third grade to incorporate language in content-area instruction. Therefore, already from the beginning of second grade, teachers need to actively expose ELL students to all kinds of informational texts so that when ELL students are expected to write from multiple sources about a single topic, ELL students would have already heard targeted language and relevant content specific to that task.

Areas of Writing

- ELL students struggle with language including word choice and the language of particular discourses for writing
- How students introduce different ideas in paragraph
- How students apply the writing structure (i.e., cause-effect, compare/contrast, description) to the writing task itself
- How students narrow ideas from general to specific

The Writing Process

- The extent to which students incorporate information from conversations and texts (students may share conversations with other groups, teachers, and the whole class to help students internalize vocabulary and concepts in the reading, discussion, and writing)
- How ELL students draw upon the linguistic and cultural knowledge to form their writing
- How ELL students appropriate the type of discourse, language, and academic vocabulary to suit various genres including personal and informational texts
- How students use the language of the teacher and the classroom
- How students use experiences and meaningful evidence to support the purpose of writing

Co-teachers can then use this expanded perspective to inform areas of assessment such as designing rubrics for written assessments as well as areas of instruction.

STRATEGIES TO SUPPORT WRITING IN CONTENT AREAS

1. Provide Opportunities for Explicit Scaffolding

English language learners often struggle in writing, and struggling writers at all levels often need some type of support to succeed. To scaffold writing tasks and activities, co-teachers can use modeling strategies that make the writing assignment feasible. For example, with modeling, co-teachers can use think-aloud, or talk about how to work through a task or solve a problem. They can also show the students examples of an expected product or provide the student with a walk-through sample of a process or a level of expectation.

Co-teachers can also use graphic organizers including charts or graphics that help students organize and record their thoughts about a topic or an idea. It facilitates and enhances comprehension and remembering. Good graphic organizers cause students to capture the essential parts of lessons, word problems, directions, notes, homework assignments, discussions, and reading passages. The examples of graphic organizers that will be illustrated in this chapter will be primarily used to compare/contrast, describe, and classify.

2. Conduct Mini-assessments That Target Writing Benchmarks and Skills

Since writing instruction is a sequential process that is not based on the student's age or grade level, but rather on her proficiency in English, determining written proficiency level is essential for planning any writing activities. For example, co-teachers can conduct an informal pre-assessment using either a writing prompt or a series of questions to determine their students' writing abilities.

3. Incorporate Effective Writing Instruction with Reading Instruction

Developing writing proficiency in the academic language of school requires multiple opportunities for ELL students to listen, speak, read, and write about academic subjects. One way co-teachers can provide ELL students with more practice with academic vocabulary in reading and writing content is to increase student-to-student interaction with academic language in all content-area classrooms. As Gibson notes, "The characteristics of effective reading instruction overlap with those of effective writing instruction" (2008).

Reading and writing share rhetorical and communicative functions, knowledge, and cognitive processes (Nelson & Calfee, 1998). ESL teachers who work with content-area teachers in their district to develop lessons and activities to enhance ELL learning will need to also help students learn how to speak, read, and write using the targeted words.

4. Increase Student Language Production

Because ELL students do not always have the language to explain their problem-solving methods, teachers need to increase student language production in the content area. Robertson (2009) suggests incorporating activities like math journals as a way for students to process what they learned and what questions they still have.

Robinson (2009) also suggests including simple prompts such as "One thing I learned today," "One thing I still don't understand . . . ," "One way I can get the help I need . . . ," and "The answer to this problem is. . . ." She points out the need to support the math skills of logic and reasoning in both reading and writing contexts when she states, "Writing out the answer to a problem is a very important skill to develop because many state math tests require a constructed response to questions."

5. Provide Opportunities for Guided Writing Instruction: Small-Group Context

Writing teachers provide effective instruction when they offer opportunities for guided writing—which is a process of collaboration. Collaboration, in this respect, is defined by a process of demonstrating, scaffolding, and modeling writing instruction whereby co-teachers collaborate with students (Gibson, 2008). As Gibson states, "Guided writing provides an important context for teachers' in-the-moment assessment and immediate instructional scaffolding of students' construction of their own, individual texts" (2008).

Furthermore, "the *guided* in guided writing lessons, then, refers to the essential nature of the support provided by expert teachers while students write" (Gibson, 2008). Since guided writing instruction is suited for a small-group context, and co-teachers already balance direct instruction with small-group work in their lessons, co-teachers can adapt Gibson's four steps to structure a twenty-minute guided writing lesson, as illustrated below:

Step #1

Teachers provide a linguistically and informationally rich activity that allows students to talk about areas of interest.

Co-teaching Recommendations
- On a planning level, co-teachers can discuss culturally appropriate and student-friendly topics. Co-teachers can bounce ideas from other content-area teachers so as to provide content-rich and relevant topics other co-teachers can use.
- Teachers can allow time to explain any difficult or challenging words or concepts.

Step #2

Teachers model a strategic behavior for writing such as a think-aloud or a cue for a strategic activity along with engaging discussions that help students integrate this strategy into their own writing.

Co-teaching Recommendations
- When using a think-aloud or talking about how to work through a task or solve a problem, co-teachers can use visual aids such as graphic organizers to assist them in their discussion. Teachers can also provide students with a walk-through sample of a process or a level of expectation or show the students examples of an expected product.

Step #3

Using strategies and prompts, teachers guide students' thinking for problem-solving while writing.

Co-teaching Recommendations
- A differentiation strategy for this step is to use student readiness as the basis of the kinds of questions teachers ask. Using Bloom's Taxonomy, co-teachers can develop sets of questions for activities and class discussion at the varying levels of challenge and difficulty.

Examples of Levels of Difficulty
- Knowledge: identification and recall of information
  - Example: who, what, when, where, how
- Comprehension: organization and selection of facts and ideas
  - Example: What is the main idea?
- Application: use of facts, rules, and principles
  - Example: How is _____ related to _____?
- Analysis: separation of the whole into component parts
  - Example: outline/diagram/web
- Synthesis: combination of ideas to form a new whole
  - Example: What would you predict/infer from _____?
- Evaluation: development of opinions, judgments, or decisions
  - Example: Do you agree with _____?

Step #4

Teachers encourage their students to share their work and, in the process, they get used to the idea of writing to a specific audience.

Co-teaching Recommendations. With shared writing, teachers can write their students' ideas on chart paper or on the board so everybody can see it. This stage may be suitable for the whole-class framework so all students can benefit. As co-teachers physically write the text, they can think aloud whatever they want their students to be thinking as they write independently.

The main focus of the shared writing is to help students see how they can communicate an idea effectively through writing. As Celic (2009) states, "For ELL students, shared writing is a wonderful way to share ideas orally, hear the language, and then see how that language connects to the written text. The vocabulary and language structures from a shared writing text can also become a model for ELLs' own writing" (p. 73). This kind of guided work can also be seen in the way ELL students take in information both orally and in writing, as illustrated in the two best classroom practices below.

Best Practices in the Classroom

While her co-teacher scaffolds the plot elements and vocabulary of a fairy tale, Ms. Grucelski uses graphic organizers with five reluctant writers over a two-week period to help them compare and contrast two fairy tales that are based on the same story but from different cultures. After mapping out the plot and discussing difficult words in context, she provides them with sentence and paragraph frames to communicate and organize their ideas. Within two weeks, they were able to write an essay.

What Does the Research Say about How ELL Students Develop as Writers?

Much of the existing research shows how ELL students build upon their linguistic knowledge in writing. As Spence (2010) states, "ELLs have particular ways of forming sentences and discourse to create meaning in their native languages, (Hickmann, 2003) which largely transfers from the native language to English writing" (Barbieri, 2002; Edelsky, 1986; Hudelson, 1986). As students are learning English, they are also taught to write according to the method of instruction and practice. "Classrooms that encourage inquiry, immersing students in examples and sounds of the genre, provide ELL students with necessary experiences" (Smith & Edelsky, 2005). ELL students need extra time to write and work with sources "even though all of the work does not show up in their writing" (Silva, 1993). As Hudelson (1999) states, ELL students should be given the following opportunities to meet their specific needs. They should be encouraged to write while they are still learning English; they should have a choice in what they write, write for a variety of purposes, and be able to use their home language resources.

SMALL MEANINGFUL WRITING TASKS IN ACTION: SENTENCE FRAMES

Many English language learners lack the cultural, linguistic, social, and emotional connection of a classroom environment. Meaningful writing tasks not only help solve the problem of cultural, social, and emotional isolation, but are also connected to real-world tasks—a concept known as authenticity. As students complete these tasks, they can immediately see how what they are learning applies to their real lives—both inside and outside the classroom.

Meaningful writing is best done on topics about which students have information and in which they have interest. For example, ready-made sentence frames help teachers identify the language structures that are critical for helping English language learners achieve competency and command of academic language. Since the strongest memories are tied to emotions, students remember better when using *I*- or *me*-type sentences because they involve them.

Sentence frames help ELL students feel more comfortable and lead them toward the responses that will be on track with the lesson. As students respond to these prompts, they can immediately see how what they are currently experiencing is connected to their own writing experience. These sentence frames may be constructed around a content-area theme or to support a specific writing strand of personal communication in which the following sentence starters may help.

Examples of "personal" sentence starters:

- "I think _____ is a superstar, because _____.
- "This new theme of _____ reminds me of a time in my life when _____."

Teachers can also ask students to make comparisons to concrete objectives in linguistic ways as illustrated in the following sentence starter:

- "I am like this _____, because I am _____."
- **Examples:** I am like this **ice-cream cone** because I am **sweet**. I am like this **red pencil** because my face is **red when I have to talk**.

Alternatively, teachers can model these sentence starters as a way to encourage student interaction. By encouraging ELL students to talk more in complete sentences, they become more proficient in writing more complete sentences.

Other Examples

Teachers write the format of the sentence they would like students to use in discussion and then hold them accountable for using it. For example, "The answer is _____ degrees because it is a _____ triangle."

Best Practices from the Classroom

To boost the confidence of their reluctant writers so that writing won't appear initially as a daunting task, Kelly and her co-teachers set a freewriting goal of how long they wanted their ELL students to write. At first, they started with three minutes, then slowly moved to four and five minutes to help build up stamina. Now they are able to write for fifteen minutes.

CO-TEACHING USING PROCESS-BASED WRITING WITH DESCRIPTION/EXPRESSION IN SCIENCE

When it comes to practicing and progressing through the stages of the writing process, ELL students need to be taught prewriting, drafting, revising, and editing successive versions. As Calderon (2011) states, "process writing can be difficult to manage when there is a wide range of students" (p. 110), which implies that a process writing approach requires co-teachers to use "elements of those strategies that seem to work better (for example, study of models, inquiry, sentence combining, writing to learn, collaborative or cooperative writing) and, most important, when vocabulary is pre-taught and students read good models of texts that contain the elements teachers want to see in their writing" (p. 110).

This instructional approach that ELL students are taught a variety of strategies ensures that they are able to also use such strategies when it comes to writing descriptive/expressive and expository/informative texts.

Since content areas of science are process-based and also require a great deal of explanation and clarification, co-teachers will need to pre-teach big content ideas prior to having students produce their own written descriptions. For example, when it comes to modeling written descriptions of types of plants—a cactus, a succulent—co-teachers will need to introduce the following big ideas in conjunction with the umbrella topic: Plants Provide Many Human Needs.

> *Big ideas*: without plants, people could not live on earth; plants give us oxygen, food, shelter, clothing, beauty, and many other things.
> Co-teachers can model the procedure using the following steps:
> *Writing mode*: descriptive/expressive
> *Content area*: science—how plants provide for human needs
> *Possible collaborative configurations*: (1) The class is divided in half and both co-teachers teach the same content to a heterogeneous group. (2) Both teachers are directing the class and are in front of the class. The core teacher teaches/models content and the ESL teacher provides examples, clarifies, uses visuals, and restates.
> *Targeted age/grade range*: early elementary, K–3

Modeling (Pre-lesson or Beginning Part of the Lesson)

Both co-teachers model and explain the descriptive/expressive writing mode. Using either a cactus, a succulent, or some other plant, the core-content or ESL teacher highlights specific nouns, adjectives, verbs, and other useful phrases such as *sounds like, smells like, feels like, reminds me of, there was a, if you see one.* As an additional lead-in, both co-teachers can ask either each other or the class the following questions about the cactus, succulent, or other plant:

- Does it have leaves? Stem? Root? Flower? Seeds?
- What is its shape? Where does it live? What can you predict about this plant?
- How would you guess it reproduces? Flower/seeds? Spores? Using a piece of itself? Why? (The exact answer is not as important as the student being able to hypothesize and give reasons.) Note: this is not directly related to the descriptive part of the writing lesson, but will be helpful when students write their own expository/informative texts.

The ESL teacher recaps words and phrases in sentences and then displays this information in a table for students.

PREWRITING AND WRITING

To anchor the descriptive part of the prewriting and writing lessons, co-teachers can engage ELL students using inquiry activities in the content areas of science and mathematics as writing for content learning "uses writing as a tool for learning content material" (Graham & Perin, 2007).

Co-teaching Using Process-Based Writing with Expository/Informative Writing

Oral

Give a student a cactus, a succulent, or some other plant and have her describe it.

- Does it have leaves? Stem? Root? Flower? Seeds?
- What is its shape? Where does it live? What can you predict about this plant?
- How would you guess it reproduces? Flower/seeds? Spores? Using a piece of itself? Why? (The exact answer is not as important as the student being able to hypothesize and give reasons.)

Written

1. Students recall the steps for changing grapes to raisins by rewriting their observations into a written report. The students take the report home for parents to read.
2. Make two charts: one in the shape of a grape, and the other in the shape of a raisin. The students write words that describe grapes and raisins on the appropriate chart.

Tips for Teaching Writing for Young, Struggling ELL Students

- Students who are unable to write may draw pictures or copy sentences.
- Ask students to select pictures and list the words that describe the pictures.
- Have students dictate the story. The student can practice reading the story and tracing the letters of individual words.
- Allow peers to write a story together. This allows students to share ideas and helps those with difficulty in writing see how others approach the task.
- Create "word banks." Ask the student to select a familiar or favorite topic. Generate a topic word list and allow the students to write about the topic for several days using the words from the bank. As a tip, create small groups to work together. Allow students to brainstorm for three to five minutes using the words in the bank. Then, the group develops a story and students help each other with structure, grammar, spelling, etc.
- Use multisensory materials to develop fine motor coordination. Students can create numbers and letters with clay, sand trays, pudding, shaving cream, tracers, and templates. Some students will need assistance and adult prompts.

REDEFINING *INFORMATIONAL TEXTS* AS AN ACADEMIC GENRE OF WRITING

The ELA/literacy shift in writing from informational sources implies that writing informational texts is an academic genre of writing and needs to be incorporated in everyday writing instruction. In fact, recognizing writing as an academic genre requires recognizing the other two literacy shifts, mainly balancing informational and literary text (shift #1) and building academic vocabulary (shift #6) since writing and reading skills also complement each other.

To accommodate these literacy shifts, teachers need to establish expectations for both co-teachers and students. Such expectations of the teacher can briefly be seen below to include the following expectations:

- Shift #5: Writing from sources
  - ELL students are required to give text-based evidence opportunities to analyze and synthesize ideas across many informational texts to draw an opinion or conclusion.
- Shift #1: Balancing informational and literary texts
  - Teachers scaffold difficulties and apply strategies so that students have the necessary content and academic knowledge to provide powerful and meaningful evidence.
- Shift #6: Building background knowledge
  - Teachers develop students' ability to use and access words that show up in everyday text and that may be slightly out of reach.

REDEFINING WRITING AS A SKILL

Addressing writing as a skill requires breaking down writing into smaller components and skills. Co-teachers will need standards to guide them in establishing objectives along with writing skills.

Best Practices from the Classroom

With her co-teacher, Kelly Grucelski maps out reading and writing standards and skills for their ELL students in the summer. In order to maintain a balance between informational/literary texts and personal narratives, she and her co-teachers reach a "compromise" that also includes a comprehensive reading and writing approach. For the first two quarters of the school year, ELL students produce poetry and personal stories, and in the third and fourth quarters, ELL students focus on expository writing—namely, writing an expository essay and a social studies report.

SCAFFOLDING STRATEGIES: WRITING ACADEMIC TEXTS

Before ELL students can write an academic text such as an essay or paragraph, co-teachers need to scaffold their ability to create that type of text in English. Academic texts include many content-specific vocabulary words and general academic words and often have a complex sentence structure. Topics are often more abstract.

Collaboration in the Development of Writing Skills 67

Examples:

1. Show students a model text, and have them identify the key language structures and vocabulary that are used. Make connections between this language and the language they've already seen in reading and in language study.
2. Have them use the vocabulary and language structures from these writing models when they begin to write their own texts.
   a. Beginning ELL students can copy parts of the writing texts in English and then illustrate their meaning. If some beginning ELLs are literate in their native language, teachers can have them write more extensively about the topic in their native language. Teachers can use their students to help with translating the final text.
   b. Intermediate and advanced ELL students can use parts of the texts to help them structure their own writing. Encourage these ELL students to use the writing models as a starting point for creating their own original texts.
3. Encourage ELL students to rehearse a story or text before beginning to draw or write it.

USING WRITTEN SENTENCE STEMS TO SUPPORT SUMMARY WRITING

Situations in which sentence stems are useful for summarizing arise during re-reading, and they also help ELL students understand key terms and main ideas.

Collaborative Strategy: Modeling Writing through Rereading Informational Texts

The literary/ELA shift #1 as part of the Common Core State Standards requires teachers to use informational and literary texts to build up academic vocabulary and knowledge and increase reading comprehension. By modeling rereading to foster students' comprehension, co-teachers can also support the writing process, especially with science and social studies passages. Scaffolding difficult texts using the technique of rereading helps teachers collaborate around the process of modeling. Both teachers work closely to teach the elements of informational texts in preparation for summary writing, as illustrated in the procedure below:

> *Targeted skills*: finding the main idea and supporting details and understanding academic vocabulary needed for full understanding of the text
>   *Collaborative configurations*: turn-taking and direct instruction
>   *Targeted age/grade range*: middle elementary
>   *Preparation of material*: preparation of sentence stems for specific sections

Planning Stage

Both teachers identify sections of an informational text that provide opportunities for guiding students toward rereading the text's main idea. This is especially challenging if the main idea does not occur in the paragraph's first or second sentence. In this case, co-teachers will be on the lookout for those striving readers who may not be able to anticipate the text's organization.

One way to support the scaffolding process that leads into writing is by having both teachers take turns modeling rereading main ideas, definitions, and their placements and whether they precede or follow key terms. "Informational text introduces, defines, and describes a large number of important terms that students must understand to find the gist of the passage" (Goldman & Rakestraw, 2000)

Modeling in Action: Explaining and Summarizing Definitions, Key Terms, and Main Ideas

In a procedure that requires rereading main ideas and definitions, co-teachers should strive for a balance between general explanations and the "nitty-gritty" of modeling and providing examples. However, before teachers can expect ELL students to write their own summaries, teachers need to first model a particular aspect of the writing process to students so they specifically see what a writer does to create a written text. In this way, they help students understand what goes through a writer's mind to compose a text.

Procedure in Action

When explaining definitions that precede key terms in informational texts, co-teachers model how to reread the sentence in such a way so that it begins with the key term. For example, a co-teacher may guide a student to complete the sentence stem in his own words.

As Hedin and Conderman (2010) suggest,

> To support [the] [student's] definition of orbit, [one] [teacher] orally model[ed] for him how to reread and restructure the sentence beginning with the key term: "An orbit is. . . ." She then guided him to complete the sentence stem in his own words ("the path planets take around the sun") after rereading the text. She then wrote the sentence stem on [the board] as she orally restated his new sentence. Finally, she thought aloud about the definition of orbit and the movement of different objects in space.
>
> Later, when thinking aloud, [the] [student] correctly used the term when talking about the moon moving around the earth. (pp. 559–560)

While the first co-teacher is illustrating a think-aloud, the second co-teacher may do one of two things:

- highlight the sentence in the paragraph and point out the definition(s); or
- use a graphic organizer to visually support what the first co-teacher is saying, as in the following:
    - An orbit is _____
    - Your new sentence: _____
    - Think of another way the moon can travel around the earth, and use it in a content-rich sentence: _____

Now that both co-teachers have scaffolded and modeled specific text features necessary for rereading, they are ready to help guide students to write their own summaries.

Scaffolding Pronoun Referents

Teachers will want to emphasize pronouns—referents that are short, decodable words that take the place of nouns in sentences. Bereiter and Bird (1985) found that comprehension improved when teachers prompted readers to "remind [themselves] what the 'referent' is—to substitute the 'real thing' for the pronoun" (p. 143).

An example of how this process works in a collaborative setting can be illustrated in the following:

Using a turn-taking model of direct instruction, co-teachers model oral and written sentence stems. For example, one teacher may model a think-aloud about pronoun referent relationships and then orally reread the preceding sentence to check for nouns that make sense in place of the pronoun. The other teacher may write sentence stems and provide explanations.

COLLABORATION IN ACTION: SCAFFOLDING SUMMARY WRITING USING RETELLING WRITING FRAMES

What Are Retelling Writing Frames?

Retelling writing frames are a scaffolded approach to summary writing. The teacher prepares a framework for students to fill in important information from the text. Students recall information after hearing or reading the text. After several readings, students retell the text using the writing frame.

Procedure in Action

Co-teacher #1

Using a graphic organizer as a visual support for rereading at the paragraph level, teacher #1 previews the passage to identify potential trouble spots, including paragraphs in which main ideas are implicit, embedded, or occur at the end of the paragraph.

Co-teacher #2

At this stage, the second co-teacher transitions into the area of scaffolding summary writing by modeling how to connect supporting details and main ideas in their summaries. At the paragraph level, graphic organizers can be used as visual supports for rereading.

As Hedin and Conderman (2010) suggest,

> Sometimes reordering sentences in writing can underscore the importance of main ideas. One method of reordering sentences is to provide readers with a photocopy of the paragraph with blank lines at the beginning. Teachers can then model for students how to write the main idea at the beginning of the paragraph. This repositioning should be followed by rereading to demonstrate how the main idea relates to the supporting details. Second, teachers can write main ideas on sticky notes or sentence stems to flexibly reposition them during rereading of original passages. (pp. 558–559)

Sample Text

> There are two ways astronomers detect planets orbiting distant stars. They measure how the stars' magnitudes, or brightnesses, and rotations change. These are clues that a planet is tugging at <u>them</u>. Comets are smaller than planets, so as they move around the sun, they often don't follow a neat path like a planet's. The four types of galaxies are classified by their shapes: *spiral, elliptical, barred, and irregular*. Long ago, many people believed Venus and Jupiter were stars, because they are two of the brightest objects in the night sky. Like the moon, these planets reflect the sun's light, but they are far from Earth. Then, about 400 years ago, the telescope was invented. It allowed people to look more closely at these planets. (Hedin and Conderman, 2010)
> <u>Underlined words</u>: pronoun referents
> *Italics*: key terms

Sample Retelling Writing Frame

> There are two ways astronomers _____ how planets can _____. First, is by _____, and ro-

tations change. These are clues that a planet is _____ at _____.

   Since comets are _____ than planets, they don't follow _____.

The four types of galaxies are classified by their shapes: *spiral, elliptical, barred,* and *irregular*. Long ago, many people believed Venus and Jupiter were stars, because they are two of the brightest objects in the night sky. Like the moon, these planets reflect the sun's light, but they are far from Earth. Then, about 400 years ago, the telescope was invented. It allowed people to look more closely at these planets.

   Galaxies have four different shapes, which include _____ _____.

   Long ago, many people believed Venus and Jupiter were _____ because they _____ _____. Like the moon, these planets show_____ _____, but they are _____ _____. Then, about 400 years ago, the telescope was invented. It ___ _____.

BRIDGING WRITING AND MATHEMATICS

Helping ELL students develop strong writing skills will eventually help them to apply writing in other contexts. Throughout the early primary grades, ELL students are expected to acquire literacy skills by listening to teachers explain their thinking about problem-solving in mathematics. Carter (2009) suggests using oral practice to create meaning through conversation about mathematical topics, which "builds their mathematical vocabulary and provides a model for them to put their own thoughts into words" (p. 608).

At the beginning stages of acquiring English, ELL students rely heavily on listening, and once teachers see that ELL students have acquired the basics, teachers can then experiment orally to help ELL students write about mathematics on a more personal level, as represented in the think-alouds on page 72. Writing about mathematics outside of math class can also help students better understand their own strategies as well as the strategies of other students. If ELL students can be taught to write detailed responses to questions and interesting essays during science or social studies, how about applying similar literacy skills in math class?

One way Carter (2009) bridges writing and math is by using sentence frames to reflect on mathematical thinking so that students would have a model for writing about mathematic thinking. "Think-alouds like these help students visualize mental processes that would otherwise be invisible" (Wilhelm, 2001).

Sentence Frames for Reflecting on Mathematical Thinking

- At first I was going to try _____, but then I decided to _____.
- I thought about what _____ said the other day and decided to try his/her strategy.
- Once I found where I got struck, I tried the problem again from the beginning. This time I decided to try _____.
- The mistake I made here was _____, and it made me think that next time I should _____.
- When I started this problem, it reminded me of _____, so I used the strategy where _____.

(Carter, 2009)

MATHEMATICAL WRITING AS AN AUTHENTIC GENRE

Authentic instruction provides students with real-life learning experiences that are connected to learning both in and out of the classroom. As Timothy Rasinski states, "Writing, like reading, is learned best when it occurs in authentic situations and for authentic purposes" (p. 618). By turning mathematical concepts and skills into an authentic lesson, teachers create a purpose and need for students to learn new skills.

Collaboration in Action

Targeted skills: finding the main idea and supporting details and understanding academic vocabulary needed for full understanding of the text
Collaborative configurations: turn-taking and direct instruction
Targeted age/grade range: early elementary, first and second grades
Preparation of material: Before helping ELL students integrate mathematical thinking in their writing, teachers build up oral practice.
Pre-lesson: direct instruction, both co-teachers teaching in front of the class
Objective: Using writing workshops to bridge math and content-area literacy

Co-teacher #1

As a springboard to the writer's workshop, the first-grade class reads together *The Doorbell Rang* (Hutchins, 1986), which is helpful for young children learning multiplication, division, and subtraction. It appeals to young children for its repetitive plot and easy-to-read style. Co-teacher #1 introduces the mathematical concept by asking the following questions:

- How many cookies are in a dozen?
- How many people can a dozen cookies be shared with?

- How would you divide twelve cookies for twelve children? Six children? Four children?

Co-teacher #1 reads the story aloud (or both teachers can divide the reading of the read-aloud) and discusses how math is handled in the story. For example, Sam and Victoria's mother makes a dozen cookies to share for two children who come home. But the doorbell rings (and rings and rings) and their cookies dwindle from twelve for two to twelve for four, to twelve for six, and finally twelve cookies for twelve children.

At each point of the story, co-teacher #1 asks: "How should the cookies be divided?" while modeling a think-aloud using a pie chart to show the actual problem-solving of the division. Co-teacher #2 can support this process by providing additional examples and illustrations.

As a next step, teachers and students can integrate white boards, and students illustrate the division of cookies and the resulting equation as they proceed through the story. Showing how they reached the answer for each problem-solving scenario is necessary for building oral and written competence, as illustrated in *Principles and Standards for School Mathematics* (National Council of Teachers of Mathematics, 2000).

As Carter (2009) points out, "By second grade, students have grasped the idea that the story is contained in the text, not the illustrations. In contrast, during math class students are encouraged to draw symbols or sketches to demonstrate problem-solving skills (NCTM, 2000). The math is contained in the pictures" (p. 608).

Alternative Role for Co-teacher #2

Co-teacher #2 provides examples and visual illustrations to support academic and content vocabulary. In *The Doorbell Rings*, the language is relatively simple and straightforward. Therefore, ELL students most likely won't be text dependent for assistance. However, teachers must make sure ELL students are making vocabulary progress in the four language domains of listening, speaking, reading, and writing. Teachers model expectations to depict the math in the story in a more detailed way.

WHAT DOES VOCABULARY INSTRUCTION LOOK LIKE IN A CO-TEACHING MATHEMATICS CLASSROOM?

To support both co-teachers' endeavor of vocabulary instruction, they may need to review best practices in vocabulary instruction. Pierce and Fontaine (2009) recommend identifying math vocabulary words and then applying research-based "tried and true" principles for vocabulary instruction in the mathematics classroom and across content areas, as discussed in this chapter and others.

The principles of robust vocabulary instruction recommended for the language arts can be successfully applied to the domain of mathematics as well. If ELL students are to be able to perform with vocabulary demands on a high-stakes math test, co-teachers need to be able to identify the words that present the greatest challenge for students, and provide opportunities for ELL students to use the words in both a reading and writing context.

Munroe and Panchyshyn (1995) referred to these two categories of mathematics vocabulary as *technical* and *subtechnical,* respectively. Technical words have a precise mathematical denotation that must be taught explicitly to students (e.g., *parallel*, *isosceles*). "Subtechnical words have a common meaning that students generally know already; however, they also have a less common, mathematical denotation that may be less familiar to students (e.g., mean, table). This ambiguity of meaning can be difficult for students" (Pierce & Fontaine, 2009).

Other examples of subtechnical words where the definition in everyday language is vastly different than the definitions in mathematics problems include: *key, pattern, rule, another way, area, shade, true, belongs, foot/feet, kind, match, model, order problem, result, ruler,* and *table* (Pierce & Fontaine, 2009).

The next section describes an example of what vocabulary instruction might look like in the math classroom before expecting ELL students to use targeted words in their writing and how teachers can incorporate these strategies in a co-teaching context.

Strategy #1: Offer Student-Friendly Definitions of Math Terms

When helping third-grade ELL students learn the meanings of the subtechnical vocabulary word, co-teachers can identify these words and co-design lessons that provide student-friendly definitions. Since the word *match* has a mathematical denotation that varies from its everyday common meaning (a contest, a tool for starting a fire versus two identical or similar items), co-teachers will need to deliberately make this point clear to the students. Students can offer their own definitions and co-teachers can decide the framework (either small group or direct instruction) for this stage of vocabulary instruction. Such words are also polysemous and tier-2 words and exist across all academic content areas.

Strategy #2: Encourage Deep Processing of Word Meanings

When teachers encourage deeper processing of word meanings, they provide extended opportunities to encounter words and also enrich the verbal environment of the mathematics classroom.

In a co-teaching context, both co-teachers may engage two groups of students in an exercise using number balances. Together, the students in each group evaluate a series of number sentences to determine whether their *means* or averages *match* the number sum, which is given to them on a separate card. This exercise also offers ELL students a chance to problem-solve using their knowledge of addition and division.

TRANSITION TO WRITER'S WORKSHOP

The writer's workshop provides opportunities for ELL students to write easy-to-understand stories about mathematical thinking and to also give and receive feedback. Students are encouraged to incorporate mathematics into a story and provide illustrations that will help the reader think about mathematics in a new or deeper way. Teachers will need to guide student writing by communicating expectations that their stories should follow. This idea is illustrated in the example below.

Suggested Collaborative Configuration

Two teachers work separately with equally divided heterogeneous groups. This allows them to differentiate writing for smaller groups of instruction.

Suggested Beginning

Teachers brainstorm a list of topics that are relevant to the topic and all students begin to freewrite. As a next step, students can use the organizational outline below to outline the content.

Suggested Middle

The middle part of the lesson is where the bulk of the writing happens, which might span over the duration of one to two class periods. To differentiate writing instruction, teachers can adapt already-existing activities without having to make up additional exercises. Teachers will want to decide how they want to engage their lower/middle/higher-performing groups using one or more of the differentiated teaching techniques such as group work, pair work, and individualization for each of the skills that is applicable to their curriculum and for meeting the needs of their students, as illustrated on page 76.

Same Task, Different Activities: Writing an Informational Text

Lower-performing group: Students brainstorm words that are relevant to the topic. Teachers can also provide story frames to help guide students in their writing.

Middle group: Students list sentences that are relevant to the topic.

Stronger group: free essay/story/composition

End/post-writing: In the author's chair, a student reads his story in front of his group and one co-teacher guides the students to ask questions not only about the aspects of the writing but also about how the math is handled in the story. Both groups come together and co-teachers ask the class if there were any text-to-text connections to any other mathematical concepts or ideas introduced in fiction or nonfiction texts.

Best Practices from the Classroom

For math error correction, Kelly Grucelski has created the error-correction journal, and she leads the students through filling it out. While she leads the kids through it, her math co-teacher circulates and helps the kids. The other fifth-grade math teacher, who teaches without Kelly Grucelski, also uses the error-correction journals in her math class, and she leads the activity by herself.

How to Create Error-Correction Journals: A Step-by-Step Process (Shared by Kelly Grucelski)

- Teacher writes a math problem (problems can be taken from a math textbook or standardized tests).
- Teacher solves the problem incorrectly, showing the student's work.
- Teacher writes a list of target vocabulary that students might use to give advice.
- Teacher writes sentence starters for the advice.
- Students read the problem and the incorrect solution.
- Students solve the math problem the correct way.
- Students write advice about how to fix the problem.
- Students orally share their advice with each other.

Example of sentence starters:

_____ (name of student) you got this problem wrong. You said _____, but the mean is supposed to be _____. You know that the mean can't be _____ because _____. When you did the problem, you forgot to _____. If you remember to _____ you will find that the mean is _____.

CHAPTER SUMMARY

Collaboration plays a key role in the process of understanding the dynamics in effective reading and writing instruction. Understanding of second-language-acquisition theories can also influence the dialogues and conversations teachers have about writing in a second language and ELL students' unique struggles with acquiring vocabulary and written language. During the beginning and intermediate stages of second-language acquisition, collaborating for the sake of informational texts as part of the literary shift for English language learners requires understanding the role of reading instruction.

ESL and general-education co-teaching is one type of collaborative framework teachers can use to focus on areas of content-specific vocabulary and writing instruction. Although some teachers may work more collaboratively than others, each instructional group requires different assessment practices that are contingent on ESL and ELL learning needs.

WEB SOURCES

Common Core and ELL Resources

- "Common Core Basics for ELLs" (many different resources are offered here by Colorín Colorado): www.colorincolorado.org/educators/common_core/ell
- "The Common Core Challenges for ELLs": www.nassp.org/tabid/3788/default.aspx?topic=The_Common_Core_Challenge_for_ELLs
- Free online content instruction videos: how to teach math, science and ELA to ELL students: http://ellib.stanford.edu/?q=education-377
- NYS Common Core Bilingual Standards: www.regents.nysed.gov/meetings/2012Meetings/March2012/BilingualStandardsPresentation.pdf
- Several free online videos from Stanford University on English language development, culture, content instruction, and L2 theory and policy: http://ellib.stanford.edu/?q=education-376
- Understanding the critical role of language in CCSS: http://ell.stanford.edu

Writing Resources

- Elementary writing rubric from the Arlington County (Virginia) Spanish partial-immersion program: www.cal.org/twi/Rubrics/index.html
- Ten resources for teaching writing with technology: www.edutechintegration.com/2011/03/10-resources-for-teaching-writing-with.html

REFERENCES FOR FURTHER READING

Writing Assessment

Anderson, C. (2005). *Assessing writers*. Portsmouth, NH: Heinemann.

Samway, K. D. (2006). *When English language learners write: Connecting research to practice, K–8*. Portsmouth, NH: Heinemann.

Launching a Writing Workshop

Calkins, L., and the Teachers College Reading and Writing Project. (2003). *Units of study for primary writing: A yearlong curriculum* (9 vols., 1 CD-ROM). Portsmouth, NH: Heinemann.

Calkins, L., and the Teachers College Reading and Writing Project. (2006). *Units of study for teaching writing, grades 3–5* (7 vols., 1 CD-ROM). Portsmouth, NH: Heinemann.

Davis, J., & Hill, S. (2003). *The no-nonsense guide to teaching writing: Strategies, structure, solutions*. Portsmouth, NH: Heinemann.

ACTIVITIES FOR FURTHER COLLABORATION

1. Take a look at a recent writing assignment that was distributed to ELL students. What are some general adjustments that co-teachers could make to promote analysis and synthesis of ideas across many texts to help draw an opinion or conclusion?
2. In addressing the resistance ELL students have regarding taking risks in their own writing, how can co-teachers respond to ELL students' writing that would help them improve while encouraging them to continue taking risks in their writing?

QUESTIONS FOR DISCUSSION

1. What could you do to help your students move toward informational writing?
2. What kind of administrative support would be needed in your school or district to help teachers to be more accountable for ELL students and informational writing?

REFERENCES

Bereiter, C., & Bird, M. (1985). Use of thinking aloud in identification and teaching of reading comprehension strategies. *Cognition and Instruction, 2*(2), 131–156.

Calderon, M. (2011) *Teaching reading and comprehension to English learners, K–5*. Bloomington, IN: Solution Tree Press.

Carter, S. (2009). Connecting mathematics and writing workshop: It's kinda like ice skating. *The Reading Teacher, 62*(7), 606–610. doi: 10.1598/RT.62.7.7

Celic, C. (2009). *English language learners day by day, K–6*. Portsmouth, NH: Heinemann.

Cote, N., & Goldman, S. R. (1999). Building representations of informational text: Evidence from children's think-aloud protocols. In H. van Oostendorp & S. R. Goldman (Eds.), *The construction of mental representations during reading* (pp. 169–193). Mahwah, NJ: Erlbaum.

Dale, T. C., & Cuevas, G. J. (1992). Integrating mathematics and language learning. In P. A. Richard-Amato & M. A. Snow (Eds.), *The multicultural classroom: Readings for content-area teachers*. White Plains, NY: Longman.

Gibson, S. A. (2008). An effective framework for primary-grade guided writing instruction. *The Reading Teacher, 62*(4), 324–334. doi: 10.1598/RT.62.4.5

Goldman, S. R., & Rakestraw, J. A., Jr. (2000). Structural aspects of constructing meaning from text. In M. L. Kamil, P. B. Mosenthal, P. D. Pearson, & R. Barr (Eds.), *Handbook of reading research* (vol. 3, pp. 311–335). Mahwah, NJ: Erlbaum.

Graham, S., & Perin, D. (2007*). Writing next: Effective strategies to improve writing of adolescents in middle and high schools*. New York: Carnegie Corporation of New York. Retrieved May 31, 2013, from www.aiceonline.com/Resources/Writing-Grade%204-12.pdf

Hedin, L. R. & Conderman, G. (2010). Teaching students to comprehend informational text through rereading. *The Reading Teacher, 63*(7), 556–565. doi: 10.1598/RT.63.7.3

Hickmann, M. (2003). *Children's discourse: Person, space and time across languages*. New York: Cambridge University Press.

Hudelson, S. (1986). Children's writing in ESL: What we've learned, what we're learning. In P. Rigg & D. S. Enright (Eds.), *Children and ESL: Integrating perspectives* (pp. 25–54). Washington, DC: Teachers of English to Speakers of Other Languages.

Hudelson, S. (1999). ESL writing: Principles for teaching young writers. *ESL Magazine, 2*(3), 8–10.

Hutchins, P. (1986). *The doorbell rang*. New York: Greenwillow.

Jarret, D. (1999). *The inclusive classroom: Teaching mathematics and science to English language learners—it's just good teaching*. Portland: Northwest Regional Educational Laboratory. Retrieved March 8, 2009, from http://nwrel.org/msec/just_good/8

Munroe, E., & Panchyshyn, R. (1995). Vocabulary considerations for teaching mathematics. *Childhood Education, 72*(2), 80–83.

National Council of Teachers of Mathematics. (2000). *Principles and standards for school mathematics*. Reston, VA: National Council of Teachers of Mathematics.

Nelson, N., & Calfee, R. C. (1998). The reading-writing connection. In N. Nelson & R. C. Calfee (Eds.), *The reading-writing connection* (97th yearbook of the National Society for the Study of Education, part II, pp. 1–52). Chicago: University of Chicago Press.

Otero, J. (2002). Noticing and fixing difficulties while understanding science texts. In J. Otero, J. A. León, & A. C. Graesser (Eds.), *The psychology of science text comprehension* (pp. 281–301). Mahwah, NJ: Erlbaum.

Pierce, M. E., & Fontaine, M. (2011). Designing vocabulary instruction in mathematics. *The Reading Teacher, 63*(3), 239–243. doi: 10.1598/RT.63.3.7

Rasinski, T., & Padak, N. (2009). Write soon! *The Reading Teacher, 62*(7), 618–620. doi:10.1598/RT.62.7.9

Robertson, K. (2009). Math instruction for English language learners. *Reading rockets.* Retrieved June 8, 2013, from www.readingrockets.org/article/30570

Silva, T. (1993). Toward an understanding of the distinct nature of L2 writing: The SL research and its implications. *TESOL Quarterly, 27*(4), 657–677. doi: 10.2307/3587400

Spence, L. K. "Generous reading: Seeing students through their writing." *The Reading Teacher, 63*(8), 634–642. doi: 10.1598/RT.63.8.2

Spolsky, Bernard. (1989). *Conditions for second language learning: Introduction to a general theory*. Oxford: Oxford University Press.

Wilhelm, J. (2001). Think-alouds: Boost reading comprehension. *Instructor, 111*(4), 26–28.

Index

academic language: bridging with everyday language, 34, 74; rate of acquisition, 55; scaffolding, 34; speaking activities using, 29–34; speaking skills in, 24–25. *See also* vocabulary
accuracy, 25–27
Adequate Yearly Progress (AYP), 7
administrative support, xx; and curriculum constraints, 7; methods of, 14–15; for professional development, 14; and time constraints, 5–7
Allington, R. L. A., 16, 19
atoms, instruction on, 40–41

Bloom's Taxonomy, 33, 60
Brown, Clara Lee, 10, 18
Brumfit, C., 25

Calderon, M. E., 14, 63
California, xvi
Carter, S., 71, 72, 73
CCSS. *See* Common Core State Standards
Celic, C., 60–61
Ciechanowski, K. M., 29, 38
classroom constraints: curriculum-related, 7; time-related, 5–7

collaboration: history of, 2–3; increase in, xv–xvi; integration of skills taught in, xix–xx; lack of, consequences of, 7–8; need for, xv, xvi, 3, 4–5, 19; obstacles to, 1, 5–7; present-day, 3–4; and seeing the "bigger picture," xvii; in special education, 2–3. *See also* co-teaching
collaborative models: definition of, 8; for ELLs, 8–9; group, 12, 13; inclusion, 17; parallel teaching, 12–13; pull-out, 12; push-in, 12; for teaching energy (science concept), 37; team teaching, 11–12
Common Core State Standards (CCSS): challenges for ELLs, xvi; English-language demands in, 4; literacy/ELA shifts in, 65–66, 67; and writing skills, 55
"Communicative Methodology in Language Teaching" (Brumfit), 25
Conderman, G., 68, 70
content-area instruction: analyzing language demands before, 36–37; and CCSS, xvi; ELL-based resource platform for, 4; integrated skill approach to, xix; Cindy Kontente and, 41–42; PRC2 routines, 29–34; speaking in, 24–25, 29–34; writing

in, 56–61. *See also* math instruction; science instruction
content-area skills: integrating with language skills, xix; speaking, 24–25, 29–34; writing, 56–61
conversational skills, 24, 28–29. *See also* speaking skills
Corrado, Ean, 42
co-teaching: framework for, 9–13; methods, 10; requirements, 10. *See also* collaboration
co-teaching models. *See* collaborative models
Co-Teaching Unit/Lesson Planning Template, sample, 42, *43–45*
Curran, M. E., 16
curriculum constraints, 7

demographic changes, 4
descriptive/expressive writing, for science, 63–65
differentiated instruction, 17, 39–40
"direct consulting," 10, 18
diversity standards, 15–16
The Doorbell Rang (Hutchins), 72–73
Dove, M., 6

Education Week blog, 4
ELA/literacy shifts, 65–66, 67
Ellis, Rod, 18, 19
ELLs. *See* English language learners
ELP Standards. *See* English Language Proficiency (ELP) Standards
energy (science concept): instruction on, 37, 38–39; science and language standards on, *39*
English language learners (ELLs): background of, and writing, 54; challenges for, xi–xii; general-education teachers of, xi, xv; increase in, 4; in K-12, 15; with learning disabilities, 16–19; low achievement in, xv, 7–8; need of support, xi–xii, xvi; stakeholders in, 7; term, xxii; young (K-2), 8, 25, 35–36, 65

English language proficiency levels: differentiating instruction by, 39–40; receptive *vs.* productive, 55; written, assessing, 56, 58
English Language Proficiency (ELP) Standards, 39, *39*; failure to reach, 7–8
error analysis, 18–19
error correction, 26–27
error-correction journals, math, 76
ESL (English as a second language) (term), xxii
ESL co-teaching framework, 9–13; as "direct consulting," 10, 18
ESL team teaching, 18–19
everyday language: bridging with academic language, 34, 74; conversational skills in, 24; in math instruction, 74; rate of acquisition, 55; in science instruction, 34
expository/informative writing, for science, 63, 64–65

Fernandez, Nicole, 12
fill-in-the-blanks activities, 62; math error-correction journals, 76; retelling writing frames, 69–71; for writing and speaking, 28
fluency, 25–26
"The Fluency Paradox Revisited" (Harmer), 25
freewriting, 63
funding, 5, 7

GCF (Greater Common Factor) graphic organizer, 41, 42, *46, 47*
general-education teacher: and collaboration, xv–xvi, xix–xx; collaboration in special education, 2–3, 10; co-teaching with ESL teacher, 9–13; co-teaching with special-education teacher, 10; in inclusion model, 17; as teachers of ELLs, xi, xv
Gibson, S. A., 58, 59

Index

graphic organizers: for GCF and LCM, 41, 42, *46, 47*; for retelling writing frames, 70; for writing skills, 58
group models, 12, 13
Grucelski, Kelly, 27, 35, 41, 42, 61, 63, 66, 76
guided practice: for speaking, 26; for writing, 59–61

Hakuta, Kenji, 4
Harmer, Jeremy, 25
Hedin, L. R., 68, 70
Heskett, Tracie, 2, 9
Honigsfeld, A., 6
Hudelson, S., 61

inclusion model, 17
Individualized Education Program (IEP), 2, 3
Individuals with Disabilities Education Act (1997), 2
informational texts: rereading, 67–69; in writing instruction, 66; as writing sources, 65–66
I-type sentences, 62

Jenkins, J., 26

K-2 ELLs. *See* young ELLs
K-6 ELLs: speaking skills development in, 23–48; writing skills development in, 53–77
K-12 education, ELLs as issue in, 15
Kontente, Cindy, 41–42

language demands: analyzing, 36–37; matching ELP standards to, 39
language proficiency levels. *See* English language proficiency levels
language proficiency standards. *See* English Language Proficiency (ELP) Standards
language skills: integrating with content-area skills, xix; and math skills, 56. *See also* speaking skills; writing skills

large group/small group model, 13
LCM (Least Common Multiple) graphic organizer, 41, 42, *46, 47*
Leana, Carrie R., 6
learning disabilities, ELLs with, 16–19
Lemke, J. L., 38
lesson-planning forms: Montessori SLC Co-Teaching Unit, 42, *43–45*; for young ELLs, *36*
literacy/ELA shift(s), 65–66, 67
literacy skills. *See* reading; writing skills
Lucas, Aristea, 40

machines, notesheet on, 35, *35*
Malka, Tara, 10
map lesson, sample, 41
math instruction: error correction, 76; fifth- and sixth-grade, examples, 41; GCF/LCM graphic organizer, 41, 42, *46, 47*; vocabulary instruction in, 73–75; writer's workshop (story creation) activity, 75–76; writing in, 71–73, 75–76
math journals, 58–59; error-correction, 76
math skills, and language skills, 56
math vocabulary, 74
me-type sentences, 62
Mills, K. A., 30–31
mini-books, 28
Montessori Small Learning Community (SLC) Co-Teaching Unit/Lesson Planning Template, 42, *43–45*
"morning meetings," 27
multimodal texts, 31–32
Munroe, E., 74

narrative text structure, 30–31
National Association for Bilingual Education (NABE), 15
National Council on Accreditation of Teacher Education (NCATE), 15
National Research Council science standards, 4
No Child Left Behind Act (2001), 3
notesheets, vocabulary, 35, *35*

open-ended questions, 28–29
oral reading activities, 28; PRC2, 29–34
orbits, writing about, 68–71

Panchyshyn, R., 74
parallel teaching, 12–13; on energy (science concept), 37
partner discussion, 34
partner reading, 32; PRC2, 29–34
Pennsylvania Department of Education, 37
personal narratives, 66
"personal" sentence starters, 62
Pick-a-Plot activity, 30–31
picture concept sorts, 28
plants, writing about, 63–65
PRC2 (Partner Reading and Content, Too), 29–34
Principles and Standards for School Mathematics (National Council of Teachers of Mathematics), 56, 73
process-based writing, 63–65
professional development, 13–14
proficiency standards. *See* English Language Proficiency (ELP) Standards
pronouns, 69
push-in models, 12
push-out models, 12

Queens High School of Teaching, 42
questions: open-ended, 28–29; use of, 32–33

Rasinski, Timothy, 72
reading: oral, 28, 29–34; partner, 29–34, 32; Pick-a-Plot activity, 30–31; PRC2 routines, 29–34; rereading, 67–69; in sixth-grade science, sample activity, 40–41; and speaking skills, 24, 26; and text structures, 30–32; and writing instruction, 56, 58
reading materials, level of, 30
reordering sentences, 70
rereading, 67–69

resource constraints, 5–7
resource platform, for content-area instruction of ELLs, 4
retelling, 27; activities preparing for, 28; writing frames for, 69–71
Robertson, K., 58
Robinson, 59

Sagamore Middle School, 40
Sanchez, M., 14
Sasson, Dorit, 2
school leadership, support from. *See* administrative support
science instruction: preparation for, 36–37; process-based writing in, 63–65; sixth-grade, example, 40–41; turn-taking in, 38–39; vocabulary instruction in, 34, 35, 38–39, 40–41; vocabulary notesheets, 35, *35*
science standards, sample, *39*
second-language acquisition: error analysis for, 18–19; research *vs.* practice on, 15; silent period in, 18
sentence frames, 62; for math learning, 71–72
sentence reordering, 70
sentence stems, 67, 68–69
Shah, 16
shared writing, 60–61
silent period, 18
"Simple Machines" notesheet, 35, *35*
Slavin, R. E., 14
small groups, 13
"social capital" of teachers, investment in, 6
social language. *See* everyday language
speaking instruction, 23–48; to accelerate skills, 25–26; challenges in, 24–25; in content areas, 24–25, 29–34, *36*; error correction, 26–27; fill-in-the-blank activities, 28; guided practice, 26; lesson-planning form, *36*; mini-books, 28; open-ended questions, 28–29; oral reading, 28, 29–34; picture concept sorts,

28; PRC2, 29–34; retelling, 27; vocabulary instruction in, 28, 29–34; for young ELLs, 25, 35–36
speaking skills: accuracy and fluency of, 25–27; assessing through retelling, 27; in content areas, 24–25, 29; and reading skills, 24, 26; in young ELLs, 25, 35–36
special education: collaboration in, 2–3, 17–18; for ELLs, 16–19; inclusion model, 17
special-education teacher, 10
Spence, L. K., 54, 56, 61
Spolsky, Bernard, 55
stakeholders, 7
Standards for Reading Professionals, 15
story creation, 30–31; in math, 75
subtechnical vocabulary, math, 74
summary writing, 67; rereading for, 67–69; retelling writing frames for, 69–71

teacher teams, 18
team teaching, 11–12; ESL, 18–19
technical vocabulary, math, 74
TESOL standards: language levels in, xxii; preparation for, 36–37; sample, 39
text structures, 30–32; multimodal, 31–32
time constraints, 5–7
turn-taking, for vocabulary instruction, 38–39

"variant" language, 26–27
visual aids, 38, 60. *See also* graphic organizers
vocabulary: categorization chart, 34; everyday *vs.* academic, 24, 34, 55, 74; in math instruction, 73–75; mini-books, 28; notesheets, 35, *35*; Pick-a-Plot activity, 31; PRC2 routines for, 29–34; in science instruction, 34, 35, 38–39, 40–41; in speaking instruction, 28, 29–34; and speaking skills, 24–25; turn-taking teaching model for, 38–39

WIDA standards, preparation for, 36–37
Wilhelm, J., 71
word banks, 65
writer's workshop, in math, 75–76
writing frames, retelling, 69–71
writing instruction, 53–77; challenges in, 54–57; in content areas, 56–61; explicit scaffolding in, 57–58; fill-in-the-blanks activities, 28, 62, 69–71, 76; freewriting, 63; guided writing, 59–61; to increase language production, 58–59; informational/literary and personal texts balanced in, 66; in math instruction, 71–73, 75–76; meaningful activities in, 53, 61–63; mini-assessments, 58; for process-based science texts, 63–65; and reading instruction, 56, 58; rereading modeled in, 67–69; retelling writing frames, 69–71; scaffolding for academic texts, 66–67; sentence frames, 62, 71–72; sentence stems, 67, 68–69; shared writing, 60–61; story creation, in math, 75–76; summaries in, 67–71; for young ELLs, 65
writing process, 57
writing skills, 53–77; academic, 65–66; areas of, 57; assessing, 56, 57, 58; challenges to acquiring, 54–57; importance of, 53; and math, 71; research on developing, 61; standards for, 55

Xu, S., xi

young ELLs (K-2): knowledge needed to support, 8; speaking skills development in, 25, 35–36; writing instruction for, 65

www.ingramcontent.com/pod-product-compliance
Lightning Source LLC
Chambersburg PA
CBHW070735230426
43665CB00016B/2246